FROM
FOSTER KID
TO MILLIONAIRE
TO SONGWRITER

Robert Dennis

Fulton Books
Meadville, PA

Published by Fulton Books 2023

ISBN 979-8-88505-440-9 (paperback)
ISBN 979-8-88505-441-6 (digital)

Printed in the United States of America

To all of the foster kids in this country
I dedicate this to them in hopes that it will give them more self-esteem and determination to rise above the average and to feel respect for themselves and later be proud of who they are.
God bless you for trying.
To all the people who helped make this book possible, *thank you!*

The first thing I remember about life is living in the big log house on the outskirts off Kingston Springs with my mother; her sister, Aunt Grace; her son, Dalton. My grandmother and grandfather were there also. But I don't remember him, just his picture.

The next thing I remember taking place was a large billy goat keeping us in the house. If you went outside, he would charge at you. I went to the outside toilet, and it took a long time to get back to the house. He went away just like he came. No one knew where he came from or where he went.

The next thing I remember is me sitting on a cane-bottom chair with my feet not touching the floor. I was churning the milk in a big stand-up churn. I just pushed and pulled the dasher up and down. I was too little that I couldn't get out of the chair by myself.

The next thing I remember was sitting at the breakfast table. The coffeepot was on the stove. And Aunt Grace picked it up to pour coffee in the cups on the table. When she passed it over me, the handle came off. The coffee burned me pretty bad, and I had lots of blisters. They called the doctor, and he came to the house. They rubbed me down with lard and put me in the front room off the front porch.

I remember one time, I don't know why, when my father was there. He is blind, and I am his eyes when he goes any place. He wanted to go to Annie's Place, a rough-board speakeasy at the time. It was like a small bar made of rough lumber. My daddy liked alcohol. I don't know what they sold, but I am sure it was against the law. There was also a slot machine in the place. It had a small window with the most money I ever saw in my life at one time, at least for twenty years. They were all nickels. Later Miss Annie came to board with us at the house in town. We had moved from the big log house. I have always thought the county took it for back taxes. There were no men in the house. Just all women and children, and that was during the

Depression. No money coming in. I wonder how Annie was in business until she came to live with us. But her boyfriend was the sheriff.

One day, we had moved to what we called downtown. I don't remember moving. We were just living there. I don't remember why it was still the whole family but without my grandfather. I don't remember him. He died at the big log house.

At the downtown house, I don't remember much. But there are a few things I do remember. I don't remember Russell as a baby. Only when he was big enough to play with. I remember one day we both got a haircut. We sat on a high chair, out in the front yard. It was by the fence under a big tree. Our hair was cut by a Black man. I don't remember how old he looked. But he was grown, and it just costed a quarter. I don't know if that was for both or for each. I remember there were several outbuildings on the place and some apple trees. What I remember is all of the apple slices up on the tin roof, being dried by the sun to preserve them for eating later.

Another memory is the three-section houses across the road. That's what they were called. They were owned by the railroad, and the people living there worked for the railroad. One of my best friends lived there. Also, a Black family lived in one of them. The Black boy played with us. One day, we were all playing in the road. He had the end hook from a single tree. He walked around just jingling it, making noise. I asked him to stop, but he would not. So when he walked by me, I took it out of his hand, then I threw it over on the bank of the road. The bank was covered in honeysuckle vines. It went so deep that he couldn't find it. He slapped me. I didn't cry, and that was the end of that noise.

One of the events I won't ever forget was when my friend Joel and I were playing in the woods at the back of our house. We scraped some leaves together and was going to have us a campfire. We had some matches, but we never could get a fire started. It just happened that my cousin, Dalton, walked our way to high school, which was not very far. He saw what we tried to do and told on us. It would have been bad if we had set the woods on fire. So to make sure we didn't do anything like that again, the adults called the sheriff on us. Miss Annie was boarding with us at the time after her place had burned down. The sheriff was still her boyfriend. We were told the sheriff was coming after us. So we crawled up under the house to hide. But we were told on again. The sheriff opened the door and talked to us while wavering that big pistol. We cried and promised to never do that again, so he left us alone.

Another bad event that happened was when I was given a hatchet for Christmas that year. We had firewood stacked on the back porch. It was a raining that day, so we were playing on the porch—me, my hatchet, and bother Russell. I was just chopping the wood with my hatchet, and the wood had some mole in it. I don't know how it happened, but brother Russell got his hand on the same place of wood I was chopping. And at the same time. It so happened that I chopped off the first joint of his middle finger. Someone carried him to the doctor who lived about a mile away. He sewed up his finger. We later found the part I chopped off, then we buried it in an aspirin box. He never let me forget it. He said his finger was a weather forecaster. His finger would get cold before the weather did.

In 1939, my father who had been laid off from his job at the Tennessee workshop for the blind. Was called back to work. He had been living with all of us for some time. So we moved back to Nashville on Park Avenue. We had to live close to the workshop since he had to walk to and from work.

The other thing I remember at the town house was when we had a well closed at the back porch. It had a wood cover like a cork in a bottle, but the top split in two, so we had a lard bucket over the top of the well. Bother Russell was outside playing. The rest of us were inside. We heard the rattle of the lard bucket, so we went out to see why. The bucket was on the well. We went over to see why it rattled. Taking off the bucket, we found that brother Russell had put a puppy in the well. It was too big to go down into the well and was just stuck at the top of the well. Which was lucky for everyone. We never found out why he put that puppy in the well.

One time we lived on Thirty-Third Avenue. It was a dead-end street. We lived at the end of this street in a small new house. It didn't have running water. There was a faucet in the front yard; two or three houses got their water from that faucet. At the end of the house was a path that went two or three hundred yards to an abandoned rock quarry. We used to go down there and play. The police used it for target practice. There was a steal cable tied up at the top. We used to climb down on this cable. The wall must have been seventy-five to one hundred feet tall, and we were all six to seven years old, which was scary. Russell and I used to go cross-country to Centennial Park, which was about a mile away. We walked through the woods and across the railroad tracks and came out on the back edge of the park. Folks would not let kids do that today. This is when Helen was born in 1940.

One time, we were living in a long house. It had two families in it. One in front and we lived in the back. The back was up high as if it had been a basement, but it didn't have bad steps going up. This was where Russell and Helen had the chicken pox. The doctors said I had them, but I don't remember them. They say I couldn't have had shingles if I hadn't had the chicken pox.

The family in front had a boy about my age. We played together. One day, he had a metal airplane, and we were out front. I bet him I could outrun his airplane. I ran the length of the house. I turned around to see where his plane was. It hit me in the head, between my right ear and my eye. It made a big gash and a lot of blood. I have a scared for my head, but it was covered by hair.

The last place we lived in Nashville was on Park Avenue. It was closer to the blind workshop. The only things I remember about being there was that there were lots of pony wagons coming down the street. A person with a pony pulling a wagon of vegetables, and he would walk behind it and try to sell some vegetables. There were plenty of wagons trying to sell bananas. And some were trying to buy junk iron. That was in the early 1940s.

When I went to work at Robert Orr in 1953, I had to go by the courthouse. This is where the farmers came to sell there produce. The pony wagons were gathering there. This was before the farmer's market was built.

One street over was Charlotte Avenue. On this street was a man that sold fish bait. Us boys could and did dig up some worms and carried them up to him. It didn't matter how many we had; he would give us a nickel. If there were two of us, he would give us both a nickel. This was when we were living on Park Avenue.

The last thing I remember while living in Nashville was when we were still on Park Avenue when our parents got a divorce. For a few days we were in the home of some of their friends. I remember going to the drugstore to get a tube of toothpaste. I had to carry the empty tube in order to get another one. This was in the early days of World War II. Many items were rationed, including razor blades, tires, sugar, shoes, and gas. There used to be a movie theater in Charlotte one block away. I remember we went to the movie one time. It cost a dime. Also, one night, there was a blackout in Nashville. All of the electricity was turned off. This was a practice in order to avoid the enemy from seeing where to drop the bombs. I was scared. I slept on a folding cot behind a door. It had a bed like a feather bed, but it was filled with straw. That was the only time I ever slept on a straw bed, and I was glad.

A few days later, some woman showed up in a car. We got all of our possessions in a couple of paper bags. Then she took us to the Fresh Air Camp, a children's home ion Cheatham County. It was a two-story brick building. It was way out in the country. Nothing around it. It was like in the wilderness. A few adults were staff and a whole bunch of kids. At the beginning, the boys were on the bottom floor and the girls upstairs, with the exception of a small room at the end of the second floor. This was called the hospital because a boy with TB was confined to bed. A partition across that room made another; that's where they put my bed by myself. We were not far from where my grandmother lived in White Bluff. I was thinking I would never see her again. And it made me cry. I didn't see her again until after I had finished high school and had a job and a car.

The Fresh Air Camp was more like a big farm. They had cows, horses, hogs, and chickens, and cultivated land. They also had a laundry house down by the creek, where our clothes were washed once a week. And they were stored in the clothes closet after. We had baths and clean clothes twice a week. We just stood in front of the closet, stretched out our arms. One of the staff would place a shirt across our back to see if we could wear it. It was community property once you wore it. If your parents or someone brought you something new and you kept it until closet day, you could wear it first. But the next time you saw it, someone else would be wearing it. The only thing that was yours to keep was your toothbrush and your shoes.

The camp was a hilly place. The house set on one hill with a valley below. There was another hill on the side with a creek and a lake in between. The same creek was by the laundry. On the other hill was a spring where our water came from. The spring ran all year. There was a water pike in it. It ran into what we called a ramjet. It was a machine that pumped water up the hill, past the house, into a storage tank, then water would flow by gravity into the house. The machine pump is the only one I ever saw like it. The water would run into the pump at the same time it ran into something like a bucket. When the bucket got full, it would fall down with a hard force, pushing the water out of another container located down under the bucket. There was a rubber gasket on top of the lower container. The spring water was the same power that pushed the water up the hill. It sprayed water all around the pump when it did that. This thing operated twenty-four hours a day.

This hill wrapped around to the right, leaving a large flat space between it and the creek. At the end of the flat space was another spring. It had been walled up with a pool of water inside and a door to enclose it. This is where the milk was kept from the cows. They called it the spring house. It was very cool in there. Between the spring house and the creek we had a swimming pool. It was only operated during hot weather. The water in it came from the spring-house and was very cold. The pipes to the pool were on the top of the ground because water only flowed there in hot weather. The overflow from the pool went into the creek.

Whenever we went to eat, we had to go line up out in the hall. The dining room was across one end of the building. We had lots of tables seating six people. The oldest person at the table was head of the table. Everyone passed the plates to him. He would put some of everything on your plate. You had to eat everything on your plate. When everyone had finish eating, we would raise our hands and ask that we may be excused. Then we all left the dining room. There were lots of things I didn't like to eat. So just before mealtime, I would play on the wood pile, which was located just outside the window of the dining room. I would see what they were putting on the table. What I did not want I would tell our head person not to put any of that on my plate, so we could leave early.

Most of the children at the camp were young like us. Usually from broken families where there was no one to care for them. There were very few teenagers. The boys were required to help with the garden and milk the cows. The girls were to help in the kitchen and with the laundry. There were two people in charge. There was a woman named Pinson who did most of the business and caretaking. She lived on the left side of the hall. A man named Driver who lived on the right side of the hall, who was always threatening you for something. We didn't see much of him, which suited us.

Since we were in the wilderness, there was no one to see or a place to go. Some Sundays in the summer we went to church. There was one in Craggie Hope, a railroad stop between us and Kingston Springs. It was a shortcut down an old wagon road through the woods. One grown-up would walk with the children that wanted to go. Some even went barefoot. One Sunday, it must have been a special day, they took a two-horse wagon load of us to White Bluff, which was not too far down the Highway 70. This was during the big war in 1943. Everything was rationed. The camp only had one car a station wagon.

During the summer, the big thing for the young boys was playing marbles. I don't know where we got them. We were always playing them for keeps. One day, two of the boys got into a fight over a marble game. Then all the marbles were taken away. But that didn't stop the marble games. There were lots of big oak trees on the grounds, so instead of playing with marbles, we played with acorns. In these oak trees were flying squirrels. They didn't have wings; they had skin attached to both legs. They would just stretch them straight out to their sides and sail down from the top of the tree. One day, one landed right beside me. So I grabbed him by the tail. It bit me on the wrist. *I let it go,* the tail. This all happened in the blink of an eye. I didn't do that again.

There was another building to the right of the main building. It was much smaller. It was called the library. I don't know why I don't remember any books being in there. But it was there where we gathered on days when we couldn't play outside. Sometimes on Sunday, that's where we would have church services.

There were no medical people ever there. To keep us healthy, every night before bedtime, we had to line up in the hall and get a spoonful of cod liver oil. I don't think anyone liked it. That's where I had my last spoonful.

On Saturday nights, most kids were lined up in the hall for supper. Some were still talking in the stairwell downstairs. I was just getting ready to come down. Me and another boy started down at the same time, so I bet him I could beat him down. *I was going to slide down the stair rail.* It was a two-level stair. I got one foot over the rail, then he touched or pushed me. Lucky for me, I hit somebody across the shoulder before I hit the floor. I had to lie there a few minutes. It brought a crowd. I also busted my chin. It created a scar about three inches long. It should have had some stiches, but they just put a piece of tape over it and put me to bed.

The first day of school at the children home started off by walking a half a mile up a graveled road to catch the school bus. There must have been fifteen or twenty of us. We went by this train stop in Craggie Hope. The gravel road ran out just before crossing the Turnbull River. We went right by the house where we used to live. The schoolhouse was an old-framed building. It didn't have running water or central heat. There was a stove in every room. When I first got there, they put me in the first grade, so I told the teacher I was in the first grade last year, that I was in the second grade now. So she gave me some tests, which I passed. They sent me down to the second-grade room. It was in the same building, but you had to go through the yard to get there. There were not many children in the school. The second and third grade were in the same room. But on different sides. We both had the same teacher. She taught the second grade in the morning and the third grade in the afternoon.

The school had a dining room but no kitchen. You had to bring your lunch. The only one I remember was one day, we had a sack lunch from the home. When I opened it, I saw a sandwich of meat which I did not recognize. It turned out to be calf's tongue. I took one bite, and that was enough. It just didn't fit my taste. I don't know how the home got that. One day for some reason, we all had to go into the high school, which was one big room. All four grades met in this room at the same time. I don't know how we learned as well as we did. I guess a lot of us wanted to in those days.

I was at the home on Christmas 1942 for the only time. This was during World War II. Everything was rationed. I don't know where the money came from to run the place. For Christmas, all the kids met in the office. There was a Christmas tree. This was the only time we saw it. I don't remember singing any Christmas songs, but I would think that we did. We all got a brown paper bag with either an apple or an orange and two pieces of hard candy. But to us, Christmas was just another day.

The next year in December, I was kept from going to school one day. Then Miss Pinson told me I was going home, and I would be leaving there. I didn't know where we were going. But we didn't have a home. We got all of our belongings in two paper sacks. Then later, a lady picked us up to take us where we were going. It was a long drive from Cheatham County to Wilson County. She tried to explain how and where we would be staying. Russell and I would be located with the Bright family up on the hill. Sister Helen was to be with the young Bright family. She stayed there one night. The family had a young baby, and Helen was still a baby. They said they didn't need two babies. They were looking for an old girl to help take care of their baby. So the older Bright family agreed to take her also so that we would all be together. So started our lives in foster care, which we had never heard about. That was Friday, December 3, 1943.

Then on Saturday, Mrs. Bright took us to Donelson to buy us some clothes to wear to church on Sunday. They were a very religious family and went to church every Sunday, which was for our benefit. All the clothes we had between the three of us were in two paper sacks. So come Monday, I rode a bus to school in Juliet. By then, I was in the third grade. The third grade met in a room in the Mt.

Juliet Church of Christ. The high school had burned down a few years ago, so classes were started wherever there was space available.

I spent two class years in the church building and two years in the agriculture building. The third grade left me one memory, that's when I found out when my birthday was.

We arrived at the Bright's home before lunch. So we sat around a kitchen table. Across from me sat a man I assumed was Mr. Bright. But at supper, a different man sat there. I learned then that the man at supper was Mr. Bright, and the man at lunch was the hired farmhand. He worked for Mr. Bright three different times.

Russell and I slept in the attic with their younger son. There was no heat up there or air conditioners. There were only two small windows on hinges that swung open. They faced to the north. They didn't close very tight. The north wind could push them open. We had lots of quilts to keep us warm. When it was time to get up, we didn't stay up there very long. We put on our clothes and hurried downstairs, where there was some heat.

The first few years was mostly school and school studies. As we grew older, the working chore became more. We did bring in the coal and the wood for the fire and learned how to draw water from the well. Then we started to mow the grass and fed the chickens and gathered up eggs. I was the outside person, and Russell was the inside person. He helped wash the dishes. We both had to chop weeds in the garden. By the fourth grade, I was hunting wild game and running trout lines, skinning and selling furs of skunks, opossums, foxes, and racoons. It was a way I could earn a little money. By the fifth grade, I was feeding cows and hogs and milking cows.

In the fifth grade, I had appendicitis, so I had surgery at Vanderbilt and was there several days and out of school for two weeks.

By high school, I was acting as the hired hand. Sometimes I milked five cows before breakfast. By summer, I plowed the ground using a tractor and cultivated the crops using horses and mules and hauled hay. Being the youngest, they always put me in the loft to throw back and pack the hay down. I was shorter, which helped, but the lightest, which did not. But that meant I had to handle the whole load.

Milking the cows had its restrictions. We could never go further than we could get back home before milking time. It also kelp me from being involved in anything at school.

One year we had a real cold winter. I did some fencing around a spring, so the cows could get to some water at a spring. It was while we were out for Thanksgiving. I worked in my short sleeves because it was a warm day. The next morning when we got up, there was about six inches of snow on the ground. It was the coldest I had ever been. No engine on the farm would start. It didn't last too long. We went back to school on Monday. But the next one lasted a long time. We were out for Christmas and was supposed to go back in early January, but the weather turned into a blizzard. It rained freezing rain. We were sitting in the house and could hear limbs fall off the trees that had been heavy with ice. Everything was out. Our phone was out for three months. The electricity was out for two weeks; the temperature was down to sixteen below zero. But we did get by. The animals had to stay in the barn. Russell and I moved some feed by pulling it on a piece of tin roofing. We later played on the tin by sliding on it down the hill until it rained again and ice froze on top of the snow. Then we couldn't guide the tin. I was going down the hill, and the tin slid into me. That was my last trip.

Mrs. Lois Bright
Russel, Marie
Robert and Helen

Robert, Helen, Russel

Our father visited at the children's home

Robert Helen and Russell
with our grandmother

Patricia, Teresa, and Robert
Our 2nd House

Barbara and the girls

This generation: Lee, Evelyn, Helen, Robert, and Russell

Nick, Robert, Olivia, Nathan Cheyenne at Disney World

Erica, Nathan, Susan, Nick, Barbara, Olivia,
Victoria, Stephen, Robert at Disney World

Christmas at our house

I wasn't in any activities after school. However, both of the younger Bright children did. The only activity I was part of was the senior play. And that was at night. Mr. Bright worked for the telephone company. That took his time from home early till late. And when he had any time off, he was involved with church work. We never went anywhere on vacation or picnicking while we were there. After Mrs. Bright fell and broke her leg, she began to fish a lot. So we did get to go fishing during the summer.

During the summer, Russell and I had to pick a lot of blackberries. Sometimes we would get to sell a gallon to someone and earn a dollar. They always had to grow out in the hot sun and always were full of chigger bugs and some snakes. I made me a promise which I have kept. When I grow up, I was not going to pick blackberries.

My high school years were always the same. Up early in the morning. Milk the cows before breakfast, then go to school. Come home in the afternoon, milk the cows, feed them and the hogs, gather the eggs, then study for school before bedtime. During the summer and fall, I was busy plowing, hauling hay, and working in the garden. When I was seventeen years old, I developed asthma. I guess it was my inheritance. It took a few months to find out my problem. It got so bad that I hated to see night coming. I would wake up unable to breath. This problem plagued me for many years. It kept me from doing anything physically requiring a lot of breath. It also kept me from joining the marines. But not the Air National Guard or the army. No time and no money also kept me from having girlfriends at school. I had several after finishing school. But I was not a good prospect being a foster kid. One of my biggest birthdays was turning eighteen. I had to register for the draft. At that time, all males turning eighteen had to register for an eight-year military obligation to the government. And a surprise I was no longer a foster kid. I didn't know what was to take place and when. But I knew something would be different. I wanted to go to college and tried to arrange it, but I couldn't because I had to find a job and pay all my expenses.

After I got out of school, the first thing I had to do was get a job and earn some money. My plans were to go to college in the daytime and work at night. I couldn't do either one. All day or all night, I looked at places that operated twenty-four hours a day. I finally got a job at AVCO building airplanes, but it was a day job.

Before the army got me, a friend and I tried to join the marines reserve. We both got turned down. I had asthma; I don't remember his problem. After this, I joined the Tennessee Air National Guard just to get a little extra money which was not much. But they only paid every three months. It looked a little bigger. We met one weekend each month. Being new, all we did was a lot of marching and exercises plus classes. I didn't have a job, so I spent a lot of time in the office. They let us go to church on Sunday, and when we did, we missed lunch.

I went to the summer camp the year I was in there when they had it. It was down in Gulfport, Mississippi. They had a special troop train to carry everyone down there that wanted to go on the train. I drove down in my car. I wanted some to get around in while I was there. We were off the first weekend, so me and a couple others went down to New Orleans. We were stated in the Roosevelt Hotel and did much of nothing. We did the same thing in Gulfport, marching and classes. We were F84 reconnaissance group then. Some of the pilots practiced breaking the sound barrier while we were in classes. They were not supposed to do this, but they did. The time I spent in the National Guard helped me about five dollars a month and qualified me for no active reserve when I got out.

And that ended my plans for college. I finally got a job at the Robert Orr Company. They were a wholesale grocery distributor. I had gone by the Tennessee unemployment office. The person I saw at the office had been to Mt. Juliet High School to give some test. He remembered me and gave me the information about Robert Orr. Since it was right down the street, I went right down. I saw a man named John Cunningham; he was the vice president. He explained the job was for typing invoices for grocery orders that the salesmen sent in from their customers. I had two years of typing at school and had to do sixty words a minute to pass the course. So he had me go over to the typewriter and do a test. After I finished, he said, "Okay, you can have the job." He wanted me to start right then. But I told him I had some feed in the car, and I had to get home. He said okay.

It was Friday, so he said, "Be here Monday at seven thirty." I was. There were three of us typing and an old lady behind me using just two fingers. I was pretty fast compared to her.

It happened about lunchtime that John's father who owned the company came over to talk to me. He said, "I think John hired you too cheap at eighty cents an hour. I am going to raise you to eighty-five cents an hour." So I thanked him. I thought that was pretty good to get a raise the first day. There was another lady that sat in front of me. She didn't come in until about nine o'clock. She typed until lunch. After lunch, she wrote credit memos for the customers. She used an electric typewriter. It wasn't too long before John thought we were not getting used of the electric writer that we should, so he switched typewriters between me and her. I could really go on that electric writer.

After a few months, John thought I should be able to talk to the customers when they called in on the phone. That was a little scary for me. I didn't know what they were talking about most of the time. So I started carrying the price book home at night, so I could learn what and where items were in the book. All prices were in code, so I had to learn that next. John thought it would do me good to go to a speaking class, and we agreed Robert Orr would pay half, and I would pay half. This was a public speaking class. You had to talk in front of a crowd. It did me good. I was nervous at first. But as time went on, I could speak to any group, and I got lots of practice. My biggest crowd was about 1,500. And I enjoyed that. Many times, I was asked to speak at club member meetings; and at church, I taught Sunday school.

As my work went on, I was noticed more by the owners. Mr. Cunningham, who owned the company, seemed to like me. He was the buyer for all the Hermitage Label food products. When he was looking to buy something, he would normally have a sample sent in. We had a test kitchen. One day, he invited me to a can cutting. They were cutting beets and eating them right out of the can. So he told me to try one.

I said, "Boss, I don't like beets." He liked to be called boss.

He said, "Eat some anyway."

I still didn't like beets. But over the years, I learned to like and eat a lot of items that I hadn't eaten before.

As time went on, technology was making a lot of progress. And the typing days were coming to an end. A company in Clarksville, a grocery company like us, was going out of business. They had one of these new data machines. Robert Orr agreed to buy it, a Remington Rand Card Systems. We had a room built to put it in. It was noisy and big. To keep inventory, you had a card for every case of product in the house and every item had a code number. Salesmen had to write code numbers for every item they sold. This became a big mess. We had to get someone other than the salesman to code some of their orders, but it had to succeed. That was the new thing. We had some high school boys to come in at 5:00 a.m. to pull cards and get orders ready to be shipped that day.

Jim Hughes was in charge of the room. I was his assistant. We took turns one week at a time opening up the office to run the orders for the days. Some orders came in by bus, so I had to go by the bus station on my way in before five o'clock to pick them up. One time, the orders got lost in the bus, so I was sent back to see the customers and to retake their order. I worked in this room until the army got me.

When I finished high school and got a job, I needed transportation, so I went with Mrs. Bright to Lebanon to where she traded cars. I bought a 1947 car. It cost three hundred dollars. It lasted about one year and cost too much to keep up. So I traded it for a 1950 four-door Ford. I kept it until 1958. I put a new motor in it. I drove it to Gulfport, Mississippi. When I was in the National Guard and when I was in the army, I made one round to El Paso, Texas. I didn't earn enough money to keep it while in the army. But between high school and the army, it was very good to have a car. I was friendly with several of the girls I knew and met. Most of them were short-time affairs. There was not much to look forward to with a foster kid with nothing. I was close to one at church, but she married another. Some of the boys were married right out of school. This was keeping them out of the army. I had to work to pay all my expenses. I was serious with one other girl, but she told me no. She just wanted to be friends.

And we were even after we both were married. I guess we both got a better deal. While home on leave, I reconnected with a former friend. I got really serious with her, but I was in Texas. So we wrote letters every day until she wrote her last letter and married another man. That one really hurt for a long time. I spent the next six months in Texas before I was sent to Germany.

While I was home between where I had been and Germany, I met another young girl. We wrote letters every day. When I returned home, we dated for over a year. Then we married. This has been good for both of us. We are still married after sixty years. I was able to remain friends with both of the other girls for the rest of their lives. They both were married two times, and both died during my lifetime.

Barbara and I planned our life before we were married. We bought a house and some furniture. Only as much as we needed. We planned how we could pay for it and kept a budget and record of expenses for everything we bought. She was working at the time we married. We agreed whenever we had children, she would stay home with them. If I could earn enough to pay the bills. She has never gone back to work outside the house. We are so glad. God has been good to us.

My work at Robert Orr continued until I went in the army. I spent a year and a half in the Tennessee Air National Guard. But that did not keep the draft board from calling me up. A bus load of us went to the VA hospital for a physical. One boy couldn't take the reading test. He couldn't read, so they told him they had a different test for him. We all passed and all rated 1A, which means you are next in line.

I checked with the recruiters to see what was available.

Recognition from UID Group

My retirement party

Mr. Nelson and
Robert at meeting

Robert at one of our food shows

They lied to me twice. I was told to get in school on radar and computer repair for an antiaircraft gun. I had to sign up for three years, which I did. While in basic training, the army was recruiting two-year draftees for the program. I also explained how I had a dependent sister that I had to support. They said that was fine. She would get an allowance like all dependents. Once in the army, when I tried to get this done, I went to the office in charge. They told me that the army didn't recognize sisters as dependents. The only way she would was if I adopted her. That sounded like more problems than solutions. So I didn't, but I still had the responsibility. So I had to send half of my pay of eighty dollars a month for her support. And so did brother Russell who was in the air force. That's the third time the army lied to me. This came as a surprise. We were all three foster kids, all under Tennessee Child Services.

When I turned eighteen, I was aged out on my own. I was still with the Bright family. I just had to pay for everything for myself, including the money child services had been paying. When Russell turned eighteen, he was aged out too. And to our surprise, our younger sister was also. They said since both of us were out of school, we both can get a job and support our sister. Child services was no longer involved.

Between graduation and the army, it was all work and a little play. My intentions were to go to college. I had paid down a deposit to go to David Lipscomb. I planned to go to school during the day and to work a shift at night. I tried bard ward printing. I didn't get in there. I round up at AVCO. When I asked for a night shift, I was laid off. That was about the time the Korean war ended, so they were in no hurry to keep building airplanes. So I had to find another job. I was on my own. The Brights let me stay there. I just had to pay what the child services was paying. So I took the job in Robert Orr.

Nothing unusual took place during this time. I did a couple of foolish things. We were swimming and playing in Stones River below the bridge on Stewarts Ferry Pike. Someone bet me I couldn't swim across the river and back. I had never done that before, but I didn't back down. I did swim across and back. Once I started, there was no other choice. The water was deep.

Another foolish thing I did was along with my friend, Kenneth Castleman. We were playing in Stones River on a Sunday afternoon, up the river off Bakers Grove Road. There was an old dead tree in the water along the bank. For some reason, we decided to float on this tree to the bridge. I gave my car keys to Delbert Bright and asked him to pick us up in two or three hours. It didn't work that way. Sometimes the water was so shallow that we had to help the tree across a sandbar. We had two sticks we were using to push and guide the tree. We lost them. So now it was our hands and feet and the stream. Kenneth lied down on his chest on the front. I sat in back and leaned against a limb sticking up. This tree would turn over every so often. We both were sore from tree the turning against our skin. We only had on our bathing suits. His chest was red and so was my butt. We had planned to get to the bridge in time to go to church. But it was dark and about nine o'clock when we arrived. Half of the church was there. So were the fire department and police. I don't know how everyone knew, but they thought we might drown. We were all glad we made it and decided that it wasn't enough fun to try again.

During my working years before the army, I thought I had a girlfriend at church. She was wearing my class ring, and we had been on several dares. But one night, she gave me my ring back and said nothing. The next thing I knew, she was marrying my friend. I didn't even know she knew him. But I couldn't afford a wife, so that was all right for her, and it kept him out of the army. But the marriage didn't last. She married three times, and he married two times. But they were happy for a time.

The army recruiters convinced me to sign up for three years in order to get all they promised me. I had to be at the VA hospital on January 27, 1957, at 7:00 a.m. There was a whole busload of us. Mostly from Wilson County. We all left in the early morning. We arrived early that night at Fort Smith, Arkansas. It took two to three days to get everyone signed in to where they were going, but we got plenty of shots and a haircut. I rounded up in an artillery training unit. We marched every day everywhere we went. We were in the old barracks built in a hurry during World War II. They were just one board thick. We had a stove in the middle of the room for heat. All the beds were double stacked. We were up every day at five o'clock. I thought my legs were going to fold up while we marched. We all wore heavy boots, and I was used to wearing light shoes.

It took a lot of time to getting used to everything. I was up every day at five o'clock, got dressed, and ate breakfast, and got ready to fall out for roll call. Then we would get the surprise of the day—what we were going to do. Every day was different. Every day was cold; this was February and March. We did lots of marching everywhere we went. First we had to learn to take care of our rifles. We spent a whole week on the rifle range. We started target shooting at one hundred yards and gradually moved back to five hundred yards. I qualified. We had gas training through a big tent. We went in with gas mask on then took them off for a minute. This was only chlorine and tear gas. We had instructions on mustard and nerve gas. They would hurt you to try them.

I was selected for KP once with a day beginning at 4:00 a.m. and ending at 9:00 p.m. It was tiring work even if they left you alone. Another time I was selected for fire officer. The title didn't fit the work. After a full day of training, I and several others were given the job. We had to get up at 4:00 a.m. and go across the field to the next street then build a fire in a coal furnace in the houses for the officers' office. We had no equipment but our own matches. The first time was a little difficult, but I learned. Outside our barracks were what looked like a little doghouse. The contained little cans of oil and cleaner to clean our rifles made good fire starters along with some panels from an orange crate that I would pick up at the mess hall garbage dump. I used that every time I had to start the fire. After you got the fire going, you had to go eat breakfast and get ready for roll call by seven o'clock. They used all of the cinders from the furnace for us to crawl on.

In early March, we had one week of field training. It was really cold. We had to carry everything in our backpacks for the week. The backpack had to be horse shaped like in the movies. We had only one blanket and a sleeping bag. The sleeping bag was for summer, so it would fit on the backpack. The first night we were in the woods, it rained and snowed. We were sleeping in pup tents on the ground. I thought I would freeze. I kept all of my clothes on but my boots. The end of my bed stuck out of the end of the tent and ice froze on it. We were there for a whole week. I don't remember all that we did, but we had one night of rifle practice on the firing range. Another time when the weather was a little warmer, we had day and night training going through an obstacle course and going over a fence and crawling under barbwire, just about twelve inches above the ground, and with your rifle crawling through mud and water while keeping you rifle clean and dry while a machine gun was firing live bullets over your head. You could not raise up on your knees. You would not dare to raise your head, or you would never do it again. Those were live bullets zooming overhead. The first thing everyone did after returning to the barracks was to take a shower with their clothes on. The ground we had to crawl on was full of mud puddles. Crawling under the barbwire, you had to crawl on you back with your rifle on your stomach. There was thin mud and water going down the back if your shirt was inside out. We were all muddy. It was late at night, and we had to be clean by morning. I had to pull KP one time at Fort Smith. It ran from 5:00 a.m. to 9:00 p.m. with no break time. We had to break enough eggs to fill a thirty-gallon galvanized can. If you broke a bad one, it was in the mix before you could do anything about it.

The army runs on schedule. You had to go into summer uniform on April 1 no matter what the weather was like. We had our graduation the first or second week in April. Another rule they had was you can't wear gloves unless you wear a coat. We stood in parade wearing summer uniforms and wearing a field jacket and gloves, holding our rifles and watching the drizzling rain freeze on the barrels of our rifles while someone made speeches. We got to go home on leave the next week before we went to our next assignment.

My next assignment was in Fort Bliss in El Paso, Texas. I knew when I signed up that that's where I would go. I was going to school to study the repair of computers and radar on antiaircraft guns. It just so happened that Johnson Cook, a boy I went to school with, was drafted the same time I went into the army. We were in the same outfit at Fort Smith. We drove to El Paso in my car. It took us two days. We spent the first night in Texarkana and the second night in Midland, Texas. He was assigned to a missile testing site. They lived in Fort Bliss but worked at Alamogordo in New Mexico. That's about fifty miles north in New Mexico. There was a missile test site to the east, and we had a gun test site to the west. It was all a lot of desert. I used to haul ammo for of the guns a lot of times out this fifty miles of straight level roads. There were no hills and no curves. One place along that road had three buildings on one side of the road. The truck made a humming sound that made me sleepy, so I chewed and smoked a cigar to keep me awake. I usually had two sergeants with me; they drank vodka while I drove. They were career men. You could get a quart of Black Bear Vodka in Juarez, Mexico, for ninety cents. Smoking wasn't permitted because we had a truckload of explosives. But no one was there but us.

After finishing training school for fixing radar and computers for the antiaircraft gun, I was assigned to headquarters Battery of the 168 antiaircraft battalion never touched the guns again. I was assigned to S4, which is supply. S4 handles everything in supplies that the battalion uses. We delivered food to all of the kitchens and ammo to all the guns. Of course, I was pulling KP and was a walking guard duty. I was in the 168 my whole time in Texas. When the guns were firing, I would volunteer to drive the ambulance. You just parked it at the firing range a waited. No one bothered you. Later they reorganized the food delivery and sent me on temporary duty to group headquarters, which was the best deal I ever had. We had three trucks—one handle perishable foods, one had groceries, and one hauled bakery products bread and cakes and pies. I was the second-ranking person in the group. I got to choose first. I chose the bakery. It had to be delivered six days a week. The others should be delivered three days a week, but that meant I had no KP and no guard duty or Saturday inspections. I was assigned a driver, and we had a ton-and-a-half Chevrolet stake body truck. We couldn't pick up bread until 10:00 a.m., so we would go to the PX and watch people and drink Coke. We had to be through by two or three o'clock, so it was easygoing. I had a red-haired Mexican boy from Albuquerque,

New Mexico, named Roberto Sanchez. It was the best job I had during my whole stay in the army.

On the third day of October 1958, I received orders to go to Germany. It was short notice, so I had to get ready quick. I had to get all the shots at one time. They turned me around like a barber pole. Shots in both arms two or three times. Then in both wrists. Then I needed two more but had to wait ten days before I could take them, so they said that I should just get them when I get home. But I wasn't going home just then. I went to California to visit kinfolk. I had planned to go at Christmastime, but since I was going to Germany, I had to go now. I rode a bus out there and stayed a week. My cousin was in the air force and was stationed in San Bernardino at the time. I was there about two days before I had asthma, so I took some of my grandmother's medicine. That was the first time I had asthma since I was in the army. When I got ready to go home, my cousin got me a ride on a plane going east. They said they could get me as far as Memphis. We went as far as El Paso the first evening and landed about dark. The next morning at the airport, another solider came running out to get on the airplane. I asked him where he was going. He said Nashville, Tennessee, so I said, "I will get my bag and go with you." The piolets had been gone a week an wanted The army and the government have some odd rules. When I was home, I went by the VA hospital, where I was inducted into the army. They told me they did not vaccinate active military. I would have to go to Fort Campbell, so I just said, "Forget it." When I got to Germany, they gave me some of the same shots that I took in Texas.

When I was home on leave before going to Germany, I worked at Robert Orr for two weeks. They let me do this every time I was home on leave. I could make more money there in two weeks than I would in four months in the army. It also helped my finances. Since I was paid at the end of September, it would be the end of January before I was paid again in Germany. Before January 1959, an officer just read your name from a list and handed you the amount written by your name. You never knew what the deducts were. Starting in 1959, they gave you a pink slip of paper showing all of your income and what they were for; they also showed all of the deducts. I have mine framed and hung on the wall. When I left Texas, they gave me travel pay. When I got to Germany, they sent me a check for travel pay again. When I got paid in January, I had several back pays. Since it was the end of September when I was last paid, they also took back the travel pay they sent. My total pay came to $211. My total deducts were $210,00, so I received $1.

While I was home, I had asthma real bad. It got so bad that I couldn't even talk. I was out with a former girlfriend two nights in a row. She had to take me to the General Hospital each night for a shot of Adrenalin. I hadn't had any asthma since I left Tennessee until I got to California. I told them just to charge it to the US army. On board the ship the first night, I woke up with asthma. I went on sick call that morning. The doctor just gave me some pills.

Also while I was home, I went rabbit hunting with a friend of mine. We went to a farm of some of his kin. There I met a young girl of the family. She wrote me letters to Germany very often. When I returned home, she met me at the airport. We dated for over a year, then we married. She has been my wife now for over sixty years.

When Russell and I lived with the Brights, we slept up in the attic. It was upstairs over an old log house; the kind they built with just one big room then added more later. It had two swinging windows facing north. They just closed against the wall. We had to put chairs against them to keep the wind from blowing them open. Sometimes during the winter, snow would blow through them. There was no heat up there. We slept on feather beds and under a lot of quilts. In the summer, it was opposite. There was plenty of heat. There was no air-conditioning or ceiling, just a plain tin roof, and it really got hot. Their youngest son also slept up there.

On his first year he was going to David Lipscomb High School in Nashville, so he left early with Mr. Bright and came home with him at night. During the next two years, he went to Mt. Juliet High School. He played football and basketball, so he wasn't home so much. Plus, he had girlfriends during the last year. I was old enough to milk the cows along with him, but he wasn't there very often, so it was just me. That's morning and night. Mr. Bright put in electric lights in the barn, so I could milk before daylight and after dark, so

I could still get ready for the school bus. The son didn't finish the twelfth grade. During the summer, he had a job with the telephone company, so he kept working and got married.

When Russell got out of school, he went right into the air force. We got another big surprise. We were told by the children's services that since we both were out of school, we were no longer under their care, and we were on our own. And since we were both earning money, we could take care of our sister. With Russell going into the air force and me going into the army, it took half of our monthly pay for our sister. She was still living with the Brights and going to school. The army lied to me when I joined up. They told me she would draw a dependents allowance. But when I was in the army, I was on my own again, that the army didn't recognize sisters as dependents. I was getting eighty-three dollars a month, and Russell was getting eighty dollars, so we both sent forty dollars a month home for her until she got married.

I stayed home every time I came home on leave, which was three times. Also, when I was on leave, Robert Orr let me work there for two weeks. I made as much in two weeks as I did in four months in the army. I stayed there when I was on the way to Germany, which should have never happened. I was in the antiaircraft gun battalion. There were only three left—one was in Greenland, another one in Germany. Ours was in Texas, which was being changed to a missile unit. I was trained to be a gun repairman, which I never became. In Texas, I had only one year left in the army. The one in Germany was converted to something else but was still for an antiaircraft unit. When I got to Germany at the train station, everyone's unit was called to be picked up, except mine. Me and one other man stood there alone. The sergeant in charge asked what unit we were supposed to go and that, that unit has been dissolved; it no longer existed. It has been made into another unit and that they will call them to come and get us. Which he did. This was Sunday. We were picked up by two men in a jeep and were carried to the battalion headquarters. The men on duty there assigned us to some part of the unit. The other man with me was a cook. They signed him to repair tracks on a tank which pulled the guns. I was to replace the ammo chief who was going home, which was supposed to be a rank higher than I was. I got the job but not the rank or the pay. I did it well. I got a letter of appreciation from the captain of S4, signed by the company commander and the battalion commander. He said the paperwork for a medal or ribbon was too much and that a letter was enough. I left Texas on October 3 and was due in Fort Dix in early December. I spent part of three years in Germany and was only gone a little over twelve months. We left the US on December 9 and arrived in Frankfurt on December 20.

The ocean was rough; the ship rolled from side to side, dipping water up on one side and pouring it off on the other. We slept on a canvas laced around a frame of water pipes. We had belts to strap ourselves in, so we did not fall out when the ship rolled. Some of the guys didn't use them; we could hear them rolling into the wall during the night.

The tracks we had to pull our guns were bigger than a tank. It had a dozer blade on the front to level the ground where the gun set. And an electric generator on the back ran on gasoline to run the gun. It took two men to drive it; the one on the left did most of the driving. It ran by levers and brakes. The man on the right had a ring mount over his head for a machine gun. The track carried a nine-man crew and a three-day supply of ammo. I had three trucks assigned to me at headquarters battery and three more from the firing batteries. The first night I was there, I was awakened at about 3:00 a.m. by bells ringing. So I asked the other guys what was going on. They said it was an alert. They said we had to go to our battle stations, so he asked where I was supposed to work. "I am in S4," so I asked where was S4. He said, "Follow that man," which I did. When I got there, the first man I saw asked where my helmet was. I said, "I don't have one. I just got here."

Then he asked, "So what are you supposed to do?"

"I am the new ammo chief," I replied.

He said, "Get your truck and go to the ammo dump." Next he asked, "Where is your helmet?"

I replied, "I just got here, I don't have a helmet yet."

"Okay."

Then I asked him, "Where is the truck?"

He said, "In the motor pool."

"Where is the motor pool?" I asked.

He pointed and said, "That way. Follow that guy. He is one of your drivers."

So we went, and I found I had three trucks assigned to me, and I had to drive number twenty-three. So now I had to find out where the ammo dump was. Two of the trucks had ring mounts, and mine had no cover over the top. This was the twenty-first of December; it was cold and foggy. The windshield had frost all over it. I had to stand up to see how to drive for a while. I followed the other two trucks; we went out through the woods to the ammo dump. We parked the trucks and just waited. The guy said we didn't need to load the trucks now. We used to do that, but by the time we got them loaded, the alert was over, and we had to unload again. I thought that was a good move. It was daylight when the alert was over. That was a practice run. It happened again on New Year's Eve in the middle of the night. We only had one alert during the day while I was in Germany. There were three trucks assigned to me at headquarters and three more from the firing batteries. We only used all six during the Berlin crisis. We carried every shell that we had at the time. The driver didn't like my rules. The trucks with ring mounts carried fifty-caliber machine guns. They had been only carrying one barrel. I made them carry both barrels. I wanted to be prepared if this was the real thing. We usually missed breakfast during an alert.

Let me tell you about some of the unusual things that happened in Texas. One morning, I felt sick, so I went on a sick call. The doctor examined me and said I had the Asian flu. Then he sent me to the hospital. I was there for five days. I didn't even have a razor or a toothbrush. There was no getting ready. You just went like you were. Once your temperature got one hundred or below, they dismissed you and sent you back to your company. I felt worse when I got out than I did before I went in. When I got back to the barracks, I saw that I was on the board for guard duty. I couldn't handle that, so I went on a sick call again. The doctor assigned me to quarters for a week. I couldn't do anything or go anywhere.

Another time we were practicing firing the 3.5 bazooka rocket launcher, we were to fire two shots at the target. The first time I fired it, I got blasted in the face with the blast. I looked like I got shot in the face with a shotgun. I fired two rounds. It also happened to several other men. The practice was stopped.

Some of the problems while in Germany was when the medics picked the particles out of my face then painted me up that made me look like I had the measles. Another time was when we were practicing running out from the enemy, going down a field over obstacles through barbwire, climbing out of ditches. We were firing live ammo anywhere an enemy could be hiding. There was a whole string of us across the field. We had a rope around our waists being kept in line by someone behind us. This was so that no one would be shot. It rained in the summer, and El Paso is hot. About halfway down the field, I was in a ditch a little higher than my head. I remember reaching up to pull myself up, but I collapsed. The running and the heat and climbing was too much for my asthma, so they just hauled me back to the meat wagon. That was the end of my day. There were several others that didn't make it either. It wasn't supposed to happen. I had hauled a load of ammo for the big gun to the firing range. The ammo was in the truck and fuses had to be in a trailer. If they did not fire all of the shells, they were supposed to take the fuses out and put them back in the box.

The S4 office had to sign statement saying they were. We had to haul all the unused ammo back to the ammo dump. The men working there had to open enough boxes to see that they were all as they were when we picked them up. When got back and they opened the first box of shells, it had fuses in them. That was as far as we got. We were instructed to pull that truck and trailer to an open space for every box and put the fuses back in the metal box. It was cold and snow was on the ground, and it took half a day to get it done.

When I went to S4 in Germany, I was assigned a desk to use for my paperwork. Everything had to be recorded. The first two weeks, the man I was to replace toured me around and showed me everywhere everything was and how everything was done. The ammo dump was out in the woods. It had a fence and barbwire around.

The 510 armored outfit had their ammo in there also. There was one guard in there during the day and two guards at night. There were no lights in there. It had been used for ammo for a long time, and it the ground was sandy. So he told me there was no telling what was buried in the sand. But when we chopped weeds, if we dug up, something just buried it deeper. I was not with the group chopping weeds when someone dug up a box of fuses, not knowing to bury it deeper. He kept it out and showed it. It caused a lot of confusion and paperwork. One thing you never expected was a recall on ammo. I had two; one on anti-tank mines, which I took back to Baumholder, up in the mountains in the French section. You had to pick up the replacements first then take the recalls back later. The other time was when we had some gas masks recalled. I had a driver with a jeep and trailer. We had to take them to Frankfurt. This was a pretty big city. We knew the address but didn't know where the place was located. In Germany, they didn't have many four-way stops like we do. They have what they call a traffic circle, which what we call a roundabout. With no stopping, you just take a street that leads off the circle. When we came into Frankfurt, we came upon a circle and took the wrong street. We drove around for an hour and wound up on the same circle again. But we got it right the second time.

The routine was mostly the same every day. One day, we did have an alert. It was at about breakfast time, so we missed breakfast. The fog was so thick that we couldn't see the first man in line as we marched. We just went out in the woods and sat. I got by just smoking cigars. It was a bad day for us; the German kitchen workers quit, so we had to do our own KP. We had another alert on New Year's Eve in the middle of the night. It was wild. We were driving through the woods, and not everyone was seeing good, but we had no accidents. Another time during the day on an alert, the outfit next to us was a tank battalion, and they caught two Russians in the bushes watching them. They brought them in and questioned them and let them go. They claimed they got lost, but everyone knew they were spies. The German government let the Russians have people in the country as liaison officers, just another name for spies.

Our barracks was located about halfway between Manheim and Heidelberg. We could ride the trolley to either place. There was a stop just side of the gates, and it didn't cost very much. Mannheim still had streets from the war. The buildings we were in were left over from the war. They housed the German army with no heat or air-conditioning. They were two stories tall and two basements deep. The second basement had an escape tunnel that went about a hundred yards past our motor pool. One day when some workers were working on the roof, they found an incendiary bomb lodged behind a chimney. It had been there ever since the war and never exploded. That caused a lot of talk. The buildings were very old but still in good shape. The S4 department was just a short distance away in another building. We were the supply to the whole battalion. I had a desk where I could do the paperwork. I had to keep up with all of the ammo. I had to take inventory every month, request all that we needed then go pick it up.

The supply dump was in Baumholder up in the mountain in the French section. I don't recall how many trips I have made up there. Some of the roads were narrow. We had to have signs on all four sides of the truck, reading in English and German explosive. Most vehicles would pull over, except the big dump trucks. They knew we would never hit them on purpose, or there would have been a big bang. I had one recollection on tank mines that I had to return there. You couldn't just swap them. You had to go get the new ones first then take the recalled ones back later. That way you were never without of the item.

I don't know why I was chosen. But one night, I had to take some secret papers to the next outfit about a mile up the road. It was in the wintertime, and snow was on the road. We had in our second basement locked behind a steel door one of their secret coding machines. A message came in for the outfit up the road, and I was to take it up there. It was cold and foggy. The fog over there was so thick, you could reach out and get a handful. You couldn't see ten feet. I had a driver, and we were in a jeep. He couldn't see the road, so I had to get out and walk in front of the jeep so his lights could see me. We made the trip all right because it was too far.

Another time was when I was chosen to carry a report to Six Group Headquarters. It had to be there today. It was in the afternoon before I was told. I had a driver, and we were in a jeep. Six Group Headquarters was in Stuttgart way up the road. We went on the auto bond and got there about dark. While we were on the base, we were stopped by the MPs. They told us we only had one headlight, so we told them it was burning when we left. It was only out when it was on dim. It was too late to get it fixed, and they couldn't put us up for the night. We discussed the solution for a few minutes, then they said they would escort us to the gate, then we would be on our own. There is a way to do things by the book and then there is the way things are done. I've found that out a lot. We had two lights on bright but only one on dim. We made it back all right. We just had to send in a report about the headlight.

Once during the summer, the whole battalion went to up above Kiel, located on the coast of the Baltic Sea. They did this to practice with the antiaircraft guns by firing over the water. We were there for a month. The ammo section was busy every day delivering ammo and fuses. They had an ammo dump with a fence around it and a guard inside. We delivered ammo behind each gun they placed. At night, they had two guards in the ammo dump and two behind the guns. We left all the ammo they didn't use in place. One night, the major found out we left the fuses in place, so he made us go out of bed and go put the fuses back in the ammo dump. They were classified.

The ammo section had the job to take all the duds to the dud pit. The dud pit was a hole in the ground way out in front of each gun. That was for safety purposes in case the shell decided to explode, which they could do for no reason. We got too used to doing it, and it could have been bad. We got so used to it that we just tossed one to each other when it was our time to carry one out. The ordinance department would collect them then take them some place, pile them up, and blow them up all at one time.

The German army was practicing just a little ways down the coast from us. They were using twin forty-two guns mounted on a tank chassis, sighting by eyesight and firing all tracers. We both used some radio-controlled air targets at some time. That's a model of an airplane with a wingspan of about ten feet, a radio-controlled air target. We got first shot at it. If we missed it, the Germans would shoot it down and keep shooting it until it fell in the sea. We were shooting off the bluff out over the water. We had some strong binoculars and could see way out over the water. The Russians had a ship out there watching us fire.

This was the British section of Germany. They had quite a few troops stationed there. They didn't operate the same as we did. They had nap time from twelve until two o'clock. Many of them played soccer in place of napping. We didn't have time off for a month. Some of us got into town once while we were there. We slept in the summer barracks. No windows just shutters and no air conditioners. It wasn't all that hot since we were way up north. The British kept telling us we had better qualify. If we didn't, we would have to come back in the winter when it snowed. I asked one of them how much snow. He said about up to the edge of the roof. On the way up, we slept in some kind of barn in our sleeping bags. I don't know what town we were in. On the way back, we camped on the fair parade ground in Hamburg. We slept in our pup tents. I have a picture of me sitting in front of a mine, eating supper. For food during the trip, we had C rations of small cans of something. To heat them up, we put them on the manifold of the truck motor. You had to punch a hole in the top of the can to let the pressure out, or it would explode. Some had someone had beans and franks all over the hood.

In the middle of the summer, we had the Berlin crisis. Mr. Krushchev ordered the US out of Berlin, or he would kick us out. The US said then kick because we are not leaving. The US got ready for the kick. All of the married men had to go to battalion office and make sure their last wills were in order. Or make one. All of us single people had to put all of our civilian clothes in our lockers, lock it up, and move all into one room. Then we had to take all our military gear and load up. We carried ever bullet that we had. I had six trucks and trailers of ammo, which was a three-day supply counting what was on the tracks. We delivered ammo to every gunsight. The small arms and mines stayed with us. We were somewhere close to the French border. Our mission was defense of an airfield from low-fly-

37

ing planes, and we were in a heavy woody area. We were here for about a month in pup tents. The ammo crew was always at the outpost. It was about a half a mile to the mess tent. I had me a folding cot and slept in the back of my truck. One night, I was awakened by a live gunfire; first by a rifle then by a machine gun. It didn't last long.

The next morning, I asked the crew if they heard it.

The old sergeant said, "Yes, it was me."

So I asked him what he was doing.

"I was just looking around and came across some paratroopers. They yielded for me to halt, so they fired a few rounds," he said. "Then I fired a few rounds. That's when they turned on the machine gun."

So I asked if anyone was hit.

He said, "No."

So I said, "Then you need to go back to the firing range when we return."

We also had machine guns on our trucks and on the ground. I had the 35 rocket launcher on my truck.

One night, I woke up with a bad asthma attack, so I walked down to first aid and got a shot of Adrenalin. The doctor wasn't there, so one of the medics gave me a shot. Too much of that stuff can kill you. After the shot, both of my arms were numb. They also gave me some pills. The next morning, Capt. Smith, the S4 officer, said that if I had one more attack, he would have to send me back. But it was important that I stay; I was the one who knew about the ammo supply. He did have me moved into the tent with the officers. I got over that in a day or two.

Then one day, I had to go back to the barracks to pick up something. I don't remember what it was. I had a driver with me when we went. It was a two-day trip. So when we got to the barracks, the first thing we did was to take a hot shower, put on some civilian clothes on, and go to town. There weren't many soldiers in town.

After we had spent the night on the bank of the Rhine River, the next morning, the whole battalion crossed the river on a barge. It was a pretty big barge. We put four two-and-a-half-ton truck with a trailer on at the same time. I noticed about ten feet from the barge was a balloon. It was tied by a string to something under the water. When I asked one of the bargemen what was down there. He said an APC. That's an armored personnel carrier; it is a vehicle like a small tank but with no gun turret. They used it for carrying troops into battle and not being shot on the way. It will hold eight men plus the driver. It was supposed to be able to cross the water. The men enter into it through a back door. Something must have been wrong with this one. There was no more in the water. It's not likely that there was only one. I drove my truck on with no problems. I have been across several rivers on a barrage, including Mississippi, Tennessee, and Cumberland. It took a lifetime to get a bridge across Cumberland between Donelson and East Nashville.

In town, we mingled with German civilians, young people, men, and women. Some were around midnight. One of them suggested that we go swimming in the Rhine River. So we took off. It was still hot, and the moon was shining. Some of them had bathing suits on. The rest of us went skinny-dipping. The ryan river is one of the fastest-flowing rivers in the world. I tried to sit on the bottom, and I hit the bottom more than twenty feet downstream. When we finished with our foolish trip, we caught a taxi to take us back to the barracks. He took us to the wrong one at first. Then we told him where to take us. It was after bed check, but we weren't supposed to be there anyway. But we couldn't go through the gates. They were guarded twenty-four hours a day, so we climbed over the fence, which was no problem. It was a rock wall with barbwire on top. But it had been used so many times that the wire was mashed down. We got up the next morning, got what we came for, and returned to the woods.

Not much went on back in the woods after we returned. It was not long after that the crisis was solved. All of the political leaders agreed to leave everything as they were. We took two days to get back to the barracks. We spent the first night on the banks of the Rhine River. There were still holes in the ground from the war where bombs had fallen. I didn't realize how serious this crisis was until I was on the way home on the ship. One of the men I talked to was also out in the woods. He was a medic. They had a field hospital set up with whole blood, which meant they were expecting some casualties.

I left Mannheim on December the 28. We shipped out of Frankfurt by train and spent one night on the train. We arrived the next day at Bremerhaven Port. As we waited, me and about forty others were selected to go early to the ship. I didn't know why until we got there. We were to be MP guards for the trip. We had two shifts of four hours and would be off for twelve hours all the way to the US. The first night I was outside on the ship. It was really dark and cold. We had to turn on a flashlight to find the stairs down. After that, my post was inside a hall down below. I saw nothing but the hall. There was a group of female Women's Army Corps on that deck, they said, but they were never seen. I don't know who designed the ship, but it must have been the enemy. We were embedded down below by four decks. To get to the showers and restrooms, we had to go up four decks, cross out on in the open deck, then down two more. Coming back home, I was in the front part of the ship. The water was really rough. The front end would raise up out of the water.

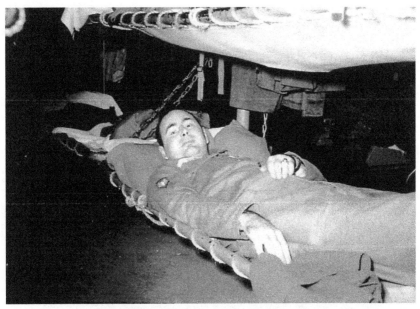

My bunk on the way to Germany

We guard a lot of sand in Texas

An old saying, "If you are
not big, have a big friend"

The Heidelberg Castle

The Germans with Twin 40s

The Arch of Triumph

In the woods during Berlin Crisis

Me and the Eiffel Tower

__ bunker at Headquarters 1 implies small arms inventory and inspect each month. I have the keys

Road sign in Germany, crazy driver

A German V1 flying bomb

Crossing the Rhine River on a barrage

Robert E. Dennis Is 'Soldier of The Month'

The letter was sent to me from the company I worked for. One of the employees saw the article in the local paper back home. I didn't know the army would put that in a local paper. I was a surprised, but it was great. They just wanted to congratulate me. My time in the army has disrupted both me and the company.

Army Specialist Four Robert E. Dennis, foster son of Mr. and Mrs. B. T. Bright, Route 4, Mt. Juliet, recently was named Soldier of the Month for the 7th Artillery in Mannheim, Germany.

An ammunition chief in the artillery's Headquarters Battery, Specialist Dennis was selected for his soldierly appearance, knowledge and performance of duties and military courtesy.

The 24-year-old soldier entered the Army in January 1957 and was stationed at Fort Bliss, Texas, before arriving overseas last December.

He was graduated from Mt. Juliet High School in 1953 and was employed by Robert Orr and Company, Nashville, before entering the Army.

45

ROBERT ORR & COMPANY
Wholesale Grocers
COFFEE ROASTERS
TELEPHONE AL 5-8333
POST OFFICE BOX 1087 • 901 SIXTH AVE., NORTH
NASHVILLE 2, TENNESSEE

October 21, 1959

ROBERT E. DENNIS
'Soldier of the Month'

We here at Robert Orr & Company are very proud
of your outstanding achievements in the performance of your duties in service to our country,
and do hereby congratulate you on this accomplishment.

John J Cunningham

Howard Nelson

Walter Cunningham

Glen Nelson Jr

Walter Cunningham

Cordell Epps

Doris Perry

William F. Owen

Dan Hicks

Robert S. Sanford

Lynne Jones

Ann Petty

Emily Robertson

Hazleton VanHook

Judy Farmer

Bill Sawyer

S. H. Wilson

R L Parker

H A Smith

J T Allen

Kathryn Hewgley

Ruby Smith

Rebecca South

Rachel VanHook

Andrew Seavy

RC Bearden

Jon Hewgley

Pauline Smith

Dale Biles

Sam Brown

Charlie Williams

Doyle Winters

HERMITAGE BRAND Fine Foods and Coffee

Hermitage
BRAND
Quality
FOODS

HEADQUARTERS
3D GUN BN (SKYSWEEPER) 7TH ARTY
OFFICE OF THE S-4
APO 28   US FORCES

3 November 1959

SUBJECT: Letter of Appreciation

THRU: Commanding Officer
          3d Gun Bn (Skysweeper) 7th Arty
          APO 28, US Forces

TO: SP4 E-4 Robert E Dennis, RA 25 355 541
          Hq Btry, 3d Gun Bn (Skysweeper) 7th Arty
          APO 28, US Forces

1. Upon my departure from this organization it is my pleasure to commend you for the outstanding manner in which you have performed your military duties as Battalion Ammunition Sergeant of this unit.

2. As Battalion Ammunition Sergeant of the unit, working in a TO&E slot authorizing a Staff Sergeant E-6, you have demonstrated exceptionally high qualities of leadership and proficiency. Your efficiency, integrity, and unselfish devotion to duty have contributed immeasurably to the success of the battalion in the accomplishment of it's mission, and to the high morale and esprit de corps of the unit.

3. Please accept my sincere appreciation and gratitude for a job well done, and may I wish you continued success in your military career.

4. A copy of this letter will be placed in your military 201 file.

EMMETT A SMITH

(3 Nov 59)   1st Ind   Lt Col McManus/dhf
SUBJECT: Letter of Appreciation

HEADQUARTERS, 3d Gun Bn 7th Arty, APO 28, US Forces, 9 November 1959

THRU: Commanding Officer, Hq Btry, 3d Gun Bn 7th Arty, APO 28, US Forces

TO: Sp4 E4 Robert E Dennis, RA 25 355 541, Hq Btry, 3d Gun Bn 7th Arty, APO 28, US Forces

I have noted with pleasure the complimentary remarks of Captain Emmett A Smith and wish to add my own expression of appreciation for the enthusiastic manner in which you have performed.

VINCENT J McMANUS
Lt Col   Arty
Commanding

(3 Nov 59)   2nd Ind   Lt Sessions/obg

Headquarters Battery, 3d Gun Bn 7th Arty, APO 28, US Forces, 13 Nov 59

TO: Sp4 E4 Robert E Dennis, RA 25 355 541, Hq Btry, 3d Gun Bn 7th Arty, APO 28, US Forces

Forwarded with pleasure, my appreciation is added to the others for your excellent performance.

JERRALD M SESSIONS
1st Lt   Arty
Commanding

47

Then it would slam back down and quiver. You thought it was going to break into. We arrived in New York harbor during the night. After we arrived in New York, we were carried back to Fort Dix by bus. We were there about two weeks, just killing time and doing odd jobs.

One day, I was folding blankets in one of the buildings. This was in January, and it was cold outside. There was a stove in the building. While I was in there, three new recruits came in to warm. The sergeant in charge asked them what they were doing. They said to warm up. He then asked them what they were doing outside. They said they were digging a hole to put a gas tank in it.

He said, "Oh, they have changed their mind. Fill the hole back up."

I thought, *I am glad I am getting out of here.*

The next day after they got all the paperwork done and paid me all the money I had coming, I was free to go. I sent my duffel bag home by train to Lebanon. That took about two weeks. I had a small bag with just what it takes to get by plus some more clothes. I caught a bus to Washing, DC. I wanted to look around while I was up here, so I did some sightseeing and spent the night. The next day, I did some more, including the White House and the Capitol Building. While at the Capitol Building, some reporter invited me to have lunch with him in the cafeteria for reporters. There was too much to see in such a short time.

The next day, I caught a bus to Roanoke, Virginia, to visit Bobbie Olsen and her daughters. They had been writing to me while I was in Germany. The girls were still in grade school. I had known them all their lives. They used to live down the road from where I was. She was married to Dough Bright, and he was the father of the two girls. He married her before he finished high school while working for the telephone company. He and I used to milk the cows. He wasn't always around at milking time. After the first girl was born and before the second one, he abandoned them and became a con man. He married women and spent their money. Then married another. He married eight times. Bobby had him drafted into the army. He stayed for a while then reenlisted to get some money. Then shot two of his fingers off to get out on a medical discharge. He ran around taking advantage of everyone he could. He drove his mother to an early grave. He drove his father to nothing. He spent everything he had to keep him out of jail. When I lived there, he had about two hundred acres. By the time he died, he was living in a trailer in the backyard of his daughters.

Brother Russell had a wife who wanted more then he could give, so she divorced him, and he moved in the trailer with Mr. Bright. After the interstate, right away came by Marie and Booty, built a bigger house that was part of the farm, and brother Russell bought their house. He lived there until he died. Russell had several different jobs at differ times. Two times he worked for me at Robert Orr. When we got a new person in charge of purchasing, he didn't like Russell, so he ran him off with a lot of other people. Russell surprised him and went to KO Lester before John knew what happened. He stayed there until he retired because of his health. They liked him very much.

After spending a few days in Roanoke, Virginia, I caught a plane home back to Mt. Juliet. Meeting me at the airport was Delbert and Jeanett Bright and Barbara Sanders. This was the girl I met on the way to Germany. She and I wrote lots of letters while I was over there. We became very interested in each other. A year and a half after, we married, but it was not sudden. We talked and planned a lot before it happened. The first thing we figured out was if we could afford it. She was working and I was working, so our plan was okay. We even bought a house before we were married. We also bought some furniture on credit, paying for it. It took a while before the deal was closed. Back then a wife's income didn't count. It was two months after we married that we were able to move in. We had more house than we had furniture. But it was our house and home.

When we married, I was working for Robert Orr, and she was working for the State of Tennessee. Neither one paid a lot of money. We had two debts—one for the house and one for the car. We paid them both. We kept a budget ledger for every dollar we spent. But money was still tight. We had our own house, but it had some empty rooms. But we had all that we needed. We stayed there for two years, then we traded it for a bigger house in Hermitage Hills. Our house payment went from eighty-six dollars to ninety-seven dollars a month. It took a lot of figuring out before we made that move. Today I still record all that we spend by category. I can tell how much it costs to live in this house or how much our cars cost to operate. And it also helps when it's time to file taxes.

We had one child when we moved to Hermitage Hills. We stayed there twelve years. We had three girls when we moved to Mt. Juliet in 1974. We only had one car when we moved to Hermitage Hills, but we had two when we moved to Mt. Juliet. One was a company car for a while before Sysco decided there would be no more company cars. They would pay you an allowance to own your own.

While we were in Hermitage Hills, we paved the driveway, put in a concrete patio, and fenced the backyard for the girls to play in. We had a swing set, a merry-go-round, and a jungle gym. All of the other children up and down the street liked to come and play with our kids. We had a full basement at the ground level with a one-car garage. I built us a den around the north end and paneled it all around. I also built a playroom for the girls between the steps and the garage to keep all their toys in. We had radiant heat coming down from the ceiling. This was good; it took up no wall space. We had three window air conditioners, so we lived in comfort.

It was a nice place to live, but the yards were small, and the houses were close together. In 1972, I bought a three-acre plot of ground in Wilson County on south Mt. Juliet Road. It was like a jungle with trees, vines, rocks, and fences. You couldn't walk through it. I paid $7,500 for it. I put two hundred down and financed it for ten years at 10 percent. I had no intention of paying it for ten years. The company had given us a super bonus for three years but not the money. They just credit it to our account, and we could get it when we needed it. So I needed it, got it, and paid it off the first year. It is almost as important to manage money as it is to make it. I never buy anything unless I know how I am going to pay for it and on time. That will always help future expenses. I spent two summers cleaning it off. It had more rocks than you could count. I spent two more years after we moved in getting rid of them.

We waited a year to get the builder that we wanted to build the house. Things don't always go as you plan. First thing, the material prices were going up so fast that he couldn't give me a price. So we agreed on cost plus 10 percent, and I got all the invoices then the delays. We want the telephone wires inside the wall, so when we requested installation, the phone company said they didn't have the manpower. Robert Orr was a big customer for the phone company and had a close friend high up in the phone company, so I asked our chairman to ask his friend if they were telling me the truth. He did then tell me to be out there at twelve o'clock to show them where to put the wires. The same thing happened again after we moved in. I was on vacation the week we moved in but had to go back on Friday and go to California that afternoon, so I called the phone company that morning. They told me it would be two months before they could get to me. Once again, I asked Mr. Bud to call his friend since I had to leave at noon. Before I went to bed that night in California, I dialed information to see if I had the phone in my house. The operator gave me the number, and I talked to my wife. I guess there are ways things are supposed to be done, then there are ways things are done. I have used that more than once in my working years.

While we were in Hermitage Hills, I bought a new Volkswagen, solid red, a 1967 model. I drove it for two years. I got thirty miles to the gallon. You could fill the tank up for three dollars. It was one of the best cars that I ever owned. I never had the spare on the ground. That's when Robert Orr furnished me a car. I had paid 1,800 for it and sold it for 1,200.

We had our new house built before we sold ours in Hermitage Hills. We got twice what we paid for. It sold in three days. When I was planning on building a new house, we got several offers from different banks wanting to loan us the money. In the meantime, we kept looking at new houses to get ideas on what we wanted to build. We wanted four bedrooms all on the same floor and on the same end of the house. There was not very many being built like that. Finally our switchboard operator told me her husband built houses, and he was building two like that right now in Brentwood. We started going over there every Sunday after church to look at those houses. We liked what we saw. He gave us a set of plans for the house, but it had a basement. We made some changes with no basement but an attached garage. Me and the builder designed the garage on a brown paper sack setting in the car out on the road. I told him I wanted it wide enough to put two cars in it and be able to open the doors on both sides and they would not touch. That's what we have and with a bonus room over them and with separate heat and air all paneled, which we call the playroom, and it's about six hundred square feet.

The road was gravel and a dead end when we moved up here. There was no traffic. Now it is paved and a state highway going from US 70 to Interstate 24. There was no bridge across Percy Priest Lake then, but it has now. And so is the shopping center in Mt. Juliet. The road is about three and a half miles up there and is four lanes wide, but sometimes during rush-hour traffic, it will back up to our driveway.

During all this time, I worked at Robert Orr. In 1972, they merged with Sysco and became a public company. Things started to change then. Before that, they had agreed to merge with Super Value in 1966, but the government interfered with that, and that deal never happened. They were a big grocery company and wanted to get in the food service business. They had the same idea that Sysco did. Sysco was all food service.

Along this time, I was really working a lot. I wound up at Mayo Clinic in Minnesota for two weeks. After seeing about ten doctors, they said all they could find was stress. They asked me to go home and not work so much. I was buying most of the private label products and taking care of the government business, which I did until the middle eighties. We built a new building in 1975 and moved into it with problems—a new computer program and changing from day loading to night loading, a new phone system, and a leaking roof. We covered our desks with sheets of plastic every night before we went home in case it rained. We rounded up with three roofs on the building before the leaking stopped. The planned floor space was too small and has been expanded and built on three times. And the floor was too low to match the floors of the trucks. But we made it work.

I did a lot of traveling in addition to working every day. I was the first national account executive at Robert Orr. They specialized in going after the chain accounts. We belonged to a marketing group in Chicago. The first big one was FW Woolworth. At that time, they were the largest food service business in the country. Bigger than the US army. I handled contact with the company and visited every store.

The group had two meetings a year in Chicago and a marketing meeting in the winter in Florida and the summer in California. One winter, we went to the Bahamas. There were many restrictions about bringing in food samples outside of the USA, so we never went outside the country again.

We did most of the business at the states of Tennessee and Kentucky. Later we did a lot with Alabama.

Mr. Glen was handling Kentucky when he became president, so he turned Kentucky over to me. He would go up to Frankfurt every three months to check all the numbers. He would fly to Louisville, rent a car, spend the day, and fly back later the same day. So when he said, "Let's go tomorrow," I would say okay. I asked if we needed some money.

He said, "I'll get the money," which he did.

We went and spent the day and met all the people in the purchasing department.

When we got back to the airport, he asked me if I had any money.

I said, "No. You were getting the money."

He said, "I did get twenty-five dollars, but I owed my wife ten dollars, which she took and one of our employees needed five dollars."

We figured what our parking costed at Nashville Airport parking lot, then we had enough money to buy one club sandwich and two Cokes for supper. I had just learned what a lot of others already knew—when with Glen, make sure you have money. From then on, when I was with him, I always brought some traveling money. He never carried money.

During the years I worked with the groups, I made many calls with them and made different presentations. I always wanted to know what kind of people I was talking to. Sometimes it was school-lunch-food people. Sometimes it was healthcare people. Sometimes it was correction people. Other times, it was public company food people or college dietician class or just a man's club. We were always discussing what was available and the cost of each and to present and save cost.

Whenever possible, Barbara went with me and helped me when she could. When working with the states, we couldn't get any credit or publicity, but we did get recognition from the government. We both were name Kentucky colonels and Tennessee colonels by the governors. Just a way of saying thank you, but no one knows about it.

In the fall after the meeting in California, I would take a week's vacation since I was already out there. I had kinfolk out in that part of the country. Barbara and the girls would come out during the meeting, and we would visit while there. When the girls were in school, we would stop over in Las Vegas, either coming or going. We would spend a day and night with my uncle and his wife, visiting them. He worked out in the Salt Flats.

While we were in the UID group, I was appointed to the product advisory committee. This group would meet with many suppliers and make judgement and decisions on which ones to do business with and which products we would buy or put our labels on. It would then be available to the whole group and in addition to how much help they could do in helping us sell it.

Once we were a part of Sysco, I was on the same type of committee for Sysco while that committee lasted in the early days. One day, when I was in the office with Mr. Nelson, we had a visiting supplier. We were a major distributor for his product. We would see him in Florida and California.

So he said, "Robert over there has been around here a long time. What is his title?"

Mr. Nelson replies, "Anything I don't want to do or haven't got time to do."

He was right, plus everything else I had to do. I guess if I was working today, they would call ne the old man from Mt. Juliet.

Some of the unusual events I remember during our trips from marketing meetings, you never knew what to expect.

One year, we had a young executive meeting in Phoenix, Arizona. I think it was more for relaxation than business. I don't remember all that went on, but the weather was really like being in an oven. Really hot. We stayed at some resort-like place. We had cabins instead of rooms. The only thing I remember well is that up the hill behind the resort was a steak house. We all had supper up there one night. It was a typical Western cowboy setting with rough lumber picnic tables inside. They cooked the steaks outside over an open-fire big grill. The cook used a long handle pitchfork like we used when we hauled loose hay. One of the real odd things were if you had on a necktie, they would cut it off then hang it on the ceiling. They had hundreds hanging up there. The food was good. Next door was some kind of a bar. People just stood around outside. Two women got into a fight. A knockdown hair-pulling, rolling-in-the-dust kind of fight. I don't know what caused it. We just stood our distance and watched it. We got to see Sen. Goldwater's big department store. It was a real nice trip for Barbara and me.

Another unusual happening happened in Florida on one meeting. Barbara and I were waiting on an elevator to go down to supper. We always had a big party on Thursday night, plus music and dancing. We were standing alone outside the elevator when the doors opened. Inside were three men. One was Sen. Henry Jackson. He was running for president. With him were two bodyguards. He invited us to ride down with them. I guess he looked and realized we were harmless. This was at the Diplomate Hotel in Hollywood, Florida.

Another unusual event happened at the Century Plaza Hotel in Hollywood, California. I had been up to Mr. Nelson's suite. He was president of our group that year, and they always provided a suite, so they could have some meetings in there. It was a big hotel and had two hallways on the floor. In a room on the other hallway was former-Pres. Richard Nixon. I was going to stop by and wish him well. All I got to see was a guard in the hallway. He stood up when he saw me coming. I guess that's what he was supposed to do.

Every summer, Mr. Nelson and friends would go up in Canada fishing, out on some lake in the wilderness. The only way in was by pontoon plane. They would stay a week and fish and whatever else they could do. Then the plane would return and take them back to civilization. I was invited to the Simplot Potato Farm and Factory in Idaho for a week. Mr. Nelson would be back on Monday, so we both were never gone at the same time. I went with Arthur Jones who was the broker for Simplot. It took all day to get there. First we had to go to Atlanta then to Dallas then to Oklahoma then to Salt Lake City then to Boise, Idaho, where we were picked up by the Simplot people. I carried a large suitcase to Caldwell, Idaho, which would be our home for a week. Arthur and I shared a room at the Sunset Motel. We went into the room, I set my luggage down, and went to the bathroom. And the phone rang.

Arthur said to me, "It's for you."

I said, "It can't be. No one knows where I am." This trip was one way for me to get some rest.

I answered, and it was Mr. Nelson.

I said, "I thought you were fishing."

He said, "We just got back in the US at International Falls, so the first phone I saw, I called information in Idaho. I knew you would be in Caldwell but didn't know where, so I asked the operator to get the yellow pages of motels and read me down the list. When she got to Sunset, I said that's it. I knew where they would put you up. I said, 'Ring that one,' so I asked the front desk if you were there. They said you just checked in, so I said ring your room. I'll be at the office next week. Call me every other day when you get a chance."

I said everything was fine. He could never pass up a phone. I'm glad we didn't have cell phones back then. I would have never got off the phone.

Mr. Nelson and some of his friends in the food business always had some get togethers during the years. Sometimes it was not convenient for him to be gone, so I went in his place. Once I went to Florida in the summer, deep-sea fishing. I liked that. We stayed in a house on the bank of the gulf. It was on a peninsula. But the road ran across the water like it was a river and had a drawbridge. The house didn't have locks on the door. We could lock the door from the inside but not from the outside. If anything wrong happened, no one could get off the land; they would just rise the bridge until they settle the problem.

We would go out on the boat at about four o'clock in the morning and again at about four o'clock in the afternoon. We took turns sitting on the seats on the boat with rod and reels. I caught three big tarpons. One got loose, and I was glad. It had worn me out before it got loose. The other two we got up to the boat before we turned them loose. Some people have them mounted. We were there just for the fun. One fellow brought in a half of a small fish; a shark got the other half. One of my friends was fishing one time and fell asleep. While he was sleeping, his friends put a bucket on the end of his line. The pull woke him up. His friends kept telling him that he had a big one. The captain of the boat moved it around, so it took a long time to pull it in. He was really excited working the line in the water. The water was holding the bucket back and moving it around. He really thought he had a big fish. It was a big laughing party when he got it up to the boat.

Another time Barbara and I got to go the Oktoberfest in Munich, Germany, courtesy of H. J. Heinz. We flew to Chicago then flew to Munich at midnight on a chartered four-engine jet. There wasn't much sleeping on the plane. All of the people on board were food people and customers of Heinz, along with some of their people. It was late in the morning when we arrived at our hotel. The first thing we did was go to bed and get some sleep; we lost a day. We were toured around all week and fed pretty good. One day, we went to Austria. We saw sights we would never had seen before. The people in the group were all customers of Heinz, so we knew many of them. It must have been a good hotel because Charlton Hester was staying there at the time. He was filming something over there. The trip home was a long one. We were twenty-two hours travelling home. We stopped in Scotland to fuel the plane. Then when we got back to Nashville, we had to go pick up our children, but it was worthwhile.

Another time, Mr. Nelson's time didn't permit him to go to the Super Bowl in Los Angeles, so Barbara and I got to make that trip. It was courtesy of Hunt Wesson. Nothing went like it was supposed to. Our plane was late getting to Dallas, so our connection was already gone. So we had to fly on a later flight. The people picked us up in LA, along with some others left with them, so we were on our own. We were to be in a Marriott Motel on a street in Hollywood, so we caught a taxi who knew where the place was. When we tried to check in, we had no reservations nor did Hunt Wesson, whose party had no reservations. We didn't know that Marriott had two hotels on this street, and we were at the wrong one. So we had to get another taxi and go to the right one. All the people that were invited were there plus a lot more. We were to be on the sixth floor, which was no problem, but only one elevator was working. So I had to take some of our luggage up and walk down and get the rest. After the long trip, we wanted to take a shower before the banquet to freshen up. After we got into the water, we found they had no soap. By suppertime, we were not happy to be there. The trip was nice, thanks to Mr. Nelson and Hunt Wesson. The ball game was close with Washington playing Miami. Barbara went back home the next day by herself. Mr. Nelson wanted me to go on up to San Francisco to see some other food people that we do business with, so I went home the day after.

I can remember some of the big deals I made for the company that made a lot of money. They were also good for the sales force and our reputation. The first one was when we had a price freeze. The IRS came in and said we owed our customer so much money. Mr. Nelson wanted to send them a check or give them a credit memo. I convinced him to have a sale. We had some overstocked items and other items we can make a big impression, which we did and everyone was happy.

Another time was when I was working with Bob Anderson. We came up with a promotion on canned ready-to-eat pudding, which was fairly new at the time. We ran it for a month and sold three truckloads. Never before or never again.

Another deal was with H. J. Heinz's rep. They had introduced school pizza—a big square pizza with gourmet flour and cheese. They were running a promotion of one dollar off, so we offered it to the salesman in the form of a silver dollar for every case sold, and you could collect the money in advance based on how many you were going to sell. If you didn't reach your goal, you had to refund the unsold amount. The dollar was to spur sales. We also discussed the fact that we were in zone two delivery area, but our kinfolk shortly to the north was in zone one, which was a dollar cheaper. I called and talked to the owner and told him about our plan. We would buy pizza in truckloads in his name. He had to put it in cold storage, which was across the street from us. He could pick his needs in a truckload price, and we would pay the bill when it arrived. I don't remember how long we ran this deal, but our kin up north received an award for the second highest sale in the country, and our sales rep got promoted to Philadelphia to Heinz Headquarters.

Back in the 1960s, Mr. Nelson and I would do all the government bids, both in Tennessee and Kentucky. We would do Kentucky ahead of time because it had to be mailed. But Tennessee we would do them on the morning; they were due at ten o'clock. He would put down the prices. I would give him the name of who won the item last time or who came in second. He wrote them down with a lead pencil, then we would give them to the secretary, and she would copy them on the state's copy in ink. I had seen a copying machine. I thought that really would be good. I lobbied for two years for us to get one, then we could fill out the bid in ink and save a lot of time and avoid any misprints. John Cunningham finally bought one. It was a liquid operating system. It took two sheets of paper, you put your copy in between them. One sheet was positive and the other was negative. All three came out wet; one sheet was your copy. They have been made much better now and cheaper and all over the place.

Another thing I was involved in was a fax machine. At the time, I was in charge of purchasing all of the supplies that we used. The national accounts had to send out lots of price sheets each month. I used to do that, and it was time-consuming, so I bought one for them. I got lots of resistance and criticism from Nashville and Houston. I told the salespeople we would be buying some more. We had three sales offices and sent lots of mail to them all the time. I could see where this would save lots of postage and time and speed up the information. It happened. By the time I retired, every office at Houston had one, and every office at the branches had one. We have sent purchase orders by fax. In our bid office we had two, one for outgoing and one for incoming. I paid $2,200 for the first one. They have gotten a lot better and a whole lot cheaper. I even have one at home—a fax and copying machine together—and a lot better than the first one I bought, which cost less than two hundred dollars.

When I was in the army, I had an instructor who taught how to defend myself. He said to stay calm and shoot the close enemy to you. I had to tell Mr. Nelson that I had a hard time telling enemies from friends now. When in the army, enemies looked different. Now all look the same. I guess the bigger the company, the more politics abound.

In my later years, I was moved around a lot just to make room for some other people. I think they would have liked me to leave but didn't want anyone else to have me, so I stayed where they had me until my retirement time. One time they had me working with the salesmen selling Christmas paper in the summer, for delivery on the first of December. We sold a truckload. It was the first and only time it was ever done. I was still the person the government people ever talked to. I guess because they knew me. I had worked with them many years, been in every state prison, except the new ones built after I retired in Tennessee and Kentucky and some in Alabama. We were not allowed in Alabama anymore. Sysco headquarters moved us out and left that for the Alabama house. So I don't think Sysco does much government business anymore.

It was a lot in my days. I worked with the purchasing departments and with each location to help make everything easier and more efficient. I received a thank you for my effort from the governor of Kentucky. He made me and my wife both Kentucky colonels. The governor of Tennessee also made both of us Tennessee colonels and also our three daughters who helped us when we had big events in the state. That was just their way of saying thank you.

I and my family used to do a lot of traveling together. We went on vacation trips in the summer. Lots of times down to Florida. Mr. Nelson had a home in Pompano, and he would let us use it in the summer if we wanted to. We took many trips over the years going down one side of Florida and returning up the other side. We went through St. Augustine, Sliver Springs. We stayed in Daytona one year and had a great time and went back up.

The west side where they put on the water skiing show. We spent time in Tampa one year and spent lots of time around Orlando. We saw all of their tourist attractions over the times. The children have been to so many places, they can't even remember all of them. One year, we went to Williamsburg, Virginia. We went through their old town place and to Six Flags another time through the one in St. Louis and one in Louisville, Kentucky, all around Los Angeles, and even to Las Vegas to visit my uncle and again after he retired in Prescott, Arizona. We spent several days in San Diego and Mexico and on a family reunion somewhere in Ohio. We used to go to Memphis a lot because the girls liked to see wrestling there and Liberty Park.

The most extensive trip took us to Hawaii for two weeks. We went to four of the islands and went through two pineapple factories. Since I was in the food business and bought pineapple from those people, they knew I was coming and surprised us when we got off the plane in Maui. When we were walking toward the baggage area, a man stepped out from behind a pillar and asked, "Are you Robert Dennis?" When I said yes, he said, "Come go with me." I didn't know what to think. Then he said, "I am from the Maui Pineapple Factory. I came to show you around." Which he did, and it was great. We had lunch, went to the pineapple fields, saw them harvesting pineapple, then to the canning plant by the only railroad in Hawaii, then by the beach. It was such a great time that we hadn't expected. We went to the big island and saw the volcano. That was a big hole in the ground. It was dormant at the time, just bubbling some spots way down there, but it was pretty scary looking into it.

Another time I carried them to Mexico City then over to Acapulco. We went on a bus between the two towns. I wanted them to appreciate what we have back there. They didn't want to go back there. We saw farmers plowing with cows and women washing clothes in the creek and pouring water on themselves to wash the clothes that they had on. We saw families live on the sidewalk in cardboard boxes. We climbed the pyramids and saw other sights, even a bullfight. Some of the people told us if we ordered chicken to eat, to make sure we saw some bones because some places served rattlesnake and called it chicken. On the way to Acapulco, we spent the night in a small town named Tasko in a motel that used to be a gold mine. It was on the side of a mountain. There was a thunderstorm, and the thunder would bounce off the sides of the valleys and hills for a long time. The girls didn't want to stay in their room. There were so many bugs in the place. It was good that we only spent one night there.

During these trips, I had to call Mr. Nelson every other day. He would talk for thirty minutes.

One year, we went to Calloway Gardens to a cabin with no phone. Whenever we came back to the cabin, there was a note on the door that says, "Call Mr. Nelson." While we were there, we saw Pres. Roosevelt's summer white house. For such a wealthy man, he sure lived simply.

For twenty years, I carried the whole family out for Christmas supper. We went to the Ohmi Hut in Smyrna, and the food was good. I thought I could take them some place where they had never been to. If they liked it, they would go back. But they didn't unless they went with me and I paid. The Ohmi Hut closed down during the virus of 2020. They couldn't get enough help to operate, which is understandable when the government is paying more not to work. So I began to taking them to the Hermitage Steak House. It cost a little more, but we get a small private room to ourselves. But it is the same process—they don't go unless it is with me and I pay. But I like to see all the small ones having a good time.

Before Barbara and I got married, we sat down and figured out if we could afford our own expenses. We decided that we could. We bought some furniture at the furniture store and put it on layaway. Barbara paid for it out of her income. I was paying the room and board plus a car payment. She had it paid for by the time we moved into our house, which we also bought before we married. It was a small house, but it was all we needed. We had one room empty after we moved in. It took about three months to get this house bought. They were always wanting me to make more money. A wife's income didn't count toward a house payment in those days. But we finally made it. Then we planned a budget each month to take care of expenses, which we never had before. We kept an account of every nickel we spent to see where the money went. Money was tight and close, but we made it without any help from anyone. I still have the ledger book that we used. The girls get a laugh at the numbers now. They laughed and said, "Mama got a new pair of shoes for three dollars." Even with a budget, there are other things to watch. Never buy anything without knowing how you are going to pay for it. There are two lists you need to make—one is for the wants, the other is for the needs. Another thought is to consider, Can I pay for it, or can I not afford it? My opinion is that every high school should teach one course one year for personal finance, covering income expenses and savings and investing. Managing your money is as important as making it. Saving to pay for an item before you buy it is important also. The world has gone crazy on charging fees for every transaction.

When I came back from the army, I went back to work for Robert Orr. Most of the people were older than I was and had more money. The men talked about their investment into an investment club, about how much money they had made. That got my interest. I asked some questions and did some research. I wound up making my first investment. I guess I was so lucky to be able to buy so little. But I think I had John Cunningham help with his friend at a local broker. I bought ten shares of Old Line Insurance Company. This is what they had been buying. It turned out good for me. It went up and split two for one. Then some bigger company bought them. I don't remember which one. By the mid-seventies, I met a stockbroker by the name of Joe Roberts. He and I worked together until he retired in 2000. He also became a good friend. I followed him through several companies. He spent most of his time with Morgan Stanley. He and they were very good for me. All three of my daughters have accounts there. He and Morgan Stanley are the reason I was able to reach over one million on net assets through my investments. All my other banking needs have been handled by the people at Pinnacle Bank. This is where I banked with these same people for many years. We never had a problem we couldn't solve in a few minutes. As a matter of fact, I don't ever remember one. They have always been good and cooperative with me. I think the most I have used them was buying new cars. They are real good people to do business with.

During the early seventies, I was awarded a stock option from Sysco. It was good for ten years, but the price was higher than the market, so it was no good. But I had a few more during the later years, which were good. The first thing I bought from Joe was Cracker Barrel. I bought it for my wife's birthday. There was nothing I could buy that she needed or that would suit her. We had agreed before we married that when we had children, she would stay home with them. She didn't have an income or spent money of her own. She didn't even have a car to go anywhere. At first, she wasn't too happy with the stock. But after she had a few more and the dividend checks were coming in more often, she liked them. I continued to buy stocks for her birthday and for Christmas. My thinking was while I was working, it would be her money. Then when I retired, it would be our money. I was wrong—it still is her money. And she looks forward to it. It may have been my best decision.

In my early years of investing, I had many things to learn. Joe was good at giving me advice. One of the things I did at his suggestion was to buy an electric utility. We bought six hundred shares for less than twenty dollars a share then reinvested the dividends. Now after I have retired and had given away over five hundred shares, I still have over three thousand shares, and they send us eight thousand dollars a year in dividends.

Since Joe retired, Caren Williams has taken his position for the whole office. She had been with him through all his years, and she does a great job. That's why I am still with Morgan Stanly. The same way with Pinnacle Bank. When it was new, I was at the grand opening. A young lady came over to me and introduced herself. She said, "I am Charice Finley, and I am your new banker. I was told to take good care of you." And she has done that for years. And I expect she will do that for many more.

At Robert Orr, for a time, I had a desk next to our treasurer. He was an older man, so I listened to his advice, but I didn't take it because I didn't have the money. One way he said I could make a profit was to go out the main road from town and look until I found where land was being sold by the frontage foot and next to it still being sold by the acre. Then buy some of the land by the acre because in a short time, it would be selling by the frontage foot. That sounded good and right, but it took more money than I could spend.

I like to buy into what is called growth and income. It may grow slower, but you can expect to receive some income along the way. I think I have all kinds, but that is my choice.

Another thing we did in my early years was to open up a margin account. This allowed me to borrow up to 50 percent on what I already owned and to buy more stock on the credit. This is not bad when the market is going up. When you can sell some of what you bought on credit and keep some of what you bought on credit, and it is paid for. As I got older, we got out of the margin business. But we did pretty good while we were in there. Besides, I just don't like credit or paying interest. But my opinion is that is what made this country great, credit on time payments.

When IRAs first became available, I signed up for me and Barbara two thousand dollars each. I put money in each year until Sysco started 401s. Then I switched to 401 because Sysco had a matching program of twenty-five cents from corporate and twenty-five cents from the local house if we reach both conditions. In the last twenty years, it failed only two times. In the twenty years, it reached the numbers only two times. Then they stared changing the numbers and have done so several times. They have also discontinued the pension program. This is the way the country is going now. I retired before the pension was dropped. It has been great for me. I rolled my IRA and 401 into one account. I didn't start taking money out until I was required. And I only take out what I have to each year. That is all I ever plan to take out. The government requires and they have their eye on every pile of money, wanting their share. It is still good, and the numbers are good.

One of the secrets to accumulate wealth is the magic of compounding. The other is to start young. I started a 401 the first year they were available and continued it to the day I retired. I never borrowed from it or took any money out until required by law.

I did make a mistake along the way. I was unhappy about paying so much income tax. It just so happened that a friend of mine told me how to reduce them. He told me to buy some rental property and had an agent call me with a good deal. This was the truth but not the whole truth, and there is a difference which is important. This is something you should always get. There is a difference between the truth and the whole truth. I didn't find out until after I sold them. I bought five duplexes all occupied. The salesman who sold them to me would manage them. This sounded really good. I took half of my investment and transferred it to real estate. Everything is not simple and easy with rental property. Everyone doesn't pay. They also move out overnight, so I had to take out more money to pay the bills. But the big problem came later. I did all the work on them that I could do. One year, I took a vacation and painted all of them on the outside. We always cleaned them up and painted the inside every time someone moved out. Over time, I had a lot of health problems, so we decided to sell them. Then I learned something else. Every year, after the write-off, we got a large tax return. The whole family enjoyed spending it. But now when my taxes were figured up, I owed forty-seven thousand dollars. This is what I wasn't told. When you sell them, you have to add back to the selling price all the money you wrote off as profit, and that is taxable. Now the deal wasn't so good. I had to borrow the money to pay my taxes. That has been the only time. I always make sure I will not be surprised at tax time. Once someone thinks you have money to spend, they will always have something you need to buy that they need to sell. I have learned to always consider who is going to benefit the most if I buy this, me or them. And most of the time, it will be them. You can watch all the advertising on TV and get the same feeling. That is something everyone needs to consider before spending their money.

I worked several different positions and jobs during my final years. I think I did well at all of them. I also think it was to keep me away from anyone else.

One of the things I have always heard is, it is good business to invest in the local community. I like that idea. I also like to have an investment in the places where I do business. I also like to know some of the people there and that they know me. I have investment in twelve companies here in Mt. Juliet and plan to buy into some more as I adjust my investments. They all are doing well and all pay dividends. We spend our money here; it's to our advantage.

I found one of the easiest ways to save money and to build wealth is to participate in a company stock purchase program. It has to be a public company and have a program, and you have to be working there. We had one at Sysco. Not from the beginning but years later. There is always a limit on how much you can buy. We were limited to 6 percent of our income and had a 15-percent discount. That can really add up over the years. Another easy way is dividend reinvestment. Both of these plans were easy, and you never got your hands on the money first. It was just like paying taxes. Your banker should also be your friend, so that he would want you to succeed in what you do. The best way to make him a friend is to do what you say you will do and do it when you say you will. That will make his accounts look good, and you and him look good. I have had good bankers all the time.

The time came when we had to get a new president at work, and it is normal they will want their own people. So I was moved around in my final years. Our first new one brought his whole family, so it was normal that they have the best positions. By the time I retired, I had worked for four of the six presidents the company had since its beginning. The first one changed my pay by reducing it 40 percent. That made a whole lot of changes in my life. I had three in college at the time. But we made changes, and the results are good today.

Those that pay dividends show that they are making money and that they have some concern for the shareholders. Those with prices in hundred dollars many pay no dividends, and the market for them is only the money manager's or funds, which put the market in the hands of too few people. Then the ordinary people can't afford to buy the high-priced stocks.

My largest and most profitable investment has been the Southern Company, an electric utility company in Georgia. Mostly because I had bought it early and they raised the dividend every year. My second largest investment has been Sysco. That's because that's where I worked, and we had employee purchasing plan with discounts. Other than these, I did pretty good in the finance area and the pharmacy area. The oil industry was pretty good, more so for dividends. You have to buy them when oil is cheap and sell them when oil is high. They do have their problems and ups and downs.

It is no secret the market trend is up, so the best way is to buy good companies and stay with them. I can remember the celebration when the DOW hit one thousand. It is now over thirty-five thousand. I used to listen to the market report on the way home from work. The NASDAQ was four hundred. It is now over fifteen thousand. I have taken a lot of money out of my investment account because my family needed it, and I hate to take on debt or pay interest. But it's just a matter of choice. That's the cause of most of our problems, making bad choices. It was a decision at the time, and everything has turned out all right.

I have never made a lot of money, but I had to take care of what I did. When I was aged out of foster care, I was on my own. Every expense was mine. There was no place to go for help. It has been that the rest of my life, and we have done all right. We have paid our bills on time and helped the children when they needed it. We have been very blessed, and I thank God every day for that. I have known people who worked all their lives and ended up with nothing. They worked, eat, drank, and gambled and had nothing. But that was their choice. I am glad that we live where we can have choices. I spent four and a half years in the military helping us have that choice. I love all people, some less than others, but I just don't understand them.

In every time period of my life, I have been fortunate enough to receive some award or some form of recognition for my work. Which was to say above and beyond the normal, I will have some of them shown in this book. In my working years, I received several from the company, also some of the places that I helped, such as the states of Kentucky and Tennessee. During my army years, I was awarded soldier of the month out of the five hundred in our unit. This time got me a three-day pass and a parade on the stand with all of the officers. Everyone else had to march by and salute us. I know all of the other guys cussed me because it interrupted their day and had to dress up for the parade.

Since I retired, I have been writing a lot of lyrics for songs, but no one has heard them. I had four published last year. I paid to have them and pitched, but I don't think the publisher told anyone about them. This year is looking a whole lot better. I may make some noise. I have had good comments but no recognition. But someday, I think I will.

I have had a good life. I can't and won't complain. Everything was not always the way I wanted it to be, but it has turned out good. I have had a lot of health problems. I have overcome them all but one. The one on my lower back. Now at eighty-seven, my wife and children say it is because they have taken good care of me. I can't deny that. I also thank God every day. I've been through the valley of death three times. One time, I had two surgeries, one after the other. I was put to sleep in both operating rooms then sent upstairs to a room and overdosed on pain medicine. I missed it all. But when I came to, there was lots of commotion going on. They told me about the excitement. I had turned blue and quit breathing. But I survived. Another time I had septic foot. I had never heard of it. That's the only time I ever went to the hospital in an ambulance. I remember getting in but didn't remember anything until the next day. I asked my daughter, Patricia, who called the ambulance and why. She is a registered nurse and has been for years. She said I wouldn't have survived any other way. Later when I was paying for my funeral, talking with Tracy Bond, she said she had seen that a lot as the cause of death on the death certificates. I woke up the next day in the ICU with four IVs in my arms and stayed a week.

The next time was when I had a heart attack. Barbara drove me down to the emergency room. They worked on me until they finally agreed I had a heart attack. The next thing I knew, I was in the ICU again. There was a lot of my family there that night. They told me all that went on, but I didn't know anything other than those three things—I have had thirty-six surgeries in my life to date and recovered from all but one. I have had two long-term problems. Years ago, when I was young, I had asthma bad. So bad at times, I couldn't talk and even when I was in the army. But it doesn't bother me much anymore. I had another long-term problem with acid reflux. I have been talking pills for it for thirty-five years. I've had several surgeries for that. The doctor used to run a scope down my throat every year to check it out. For a while, it was precancerous. But years of treatment and pills, which I am still taking, I am now the oldest man that has ever lived in our family. I thank God every day for being so good to me. I have been a conservative all my life. Always out of necessity. The only luxury that I have used for myself is a glass of Florida Natural Fresh Orange Juice each morning for breakfast, which I can afford.

Before I retired, my brother who lived about five miles down the road was diagnosed with ALS, a degenerative disease of the muscles of the body. He lived by himself, and he liked his independence. But as he got progressively worse, I had to stay in touch with him, so I got him a cordless phone and a camera case that hung around his neck, and we agreed he would call me at work every morning when he got up and every night after he went to bed. That worked fine. But one day, I didn't get a call at work, so I called him. I didn't get an answer. So I called back a few minutes; still no answer. So I left him an answer on his machine, which he could hear as I talked, telling him if he is down, just stay put, I was on the way. I left work and went to his house. I had a key to get in. He was on the floor in the bathroom. He said he had been there for about an hour. He was all right but just couldn't get up. There were several nights I got out of bed just to go get him up when he had fallen before getting into bed.

As he got worse, we had to get a sitter for him during the day. By this time, I had retired. The sitter would be with him from eight o'clock in the morning until four o'clock in the afternoon. Then I would be there until one of his sons would come to spend the night. On the weekends, he had a lady friend that would come and look after him. Holidays were a problem because his children had families. I didn't, so sometimes I was there for two or three days and nights. As he got worse, we had to grind his food and put it in his mouth. He lasted four years after the doctors decided what his problem was. But that took three years. Whoever spent the night with him slept on the couch in the living room. We had an elastic band around his arm with a doorbell button in it. We had a cordless doorbell plugged into an electric outlet. He would punch that button when he wanted someone since he could not turn over in bed by himself.

Let me tell you about me. As I was growing up, I was shy and bashful. I didn't speak up much. I felt like an outsider and didn't belong anywhere. That's a normal feeling for foster kids. After I have grown up, that has changed. I am now an American citizen with all the responsibilities and privileges; the same as everyone else. But the difference is that our foster home was very religious. We went to church three times a week. We studied the Bible. That has given us some guides on how we should live and think about what to think. My thought is the Bible is the manual for humans given by the Creator. It tells us how we should work and operate. If we follow the instructions, we would have a better world.

I grew up in the Church of Christ. I was baptized when I was thirteen and have been active all my life. When I was old enough and knew enough, I taught Sunday school to the teenagers. As I grew older, I taught the adults. I served as a director of Sunday school. I served as a deacon and as an elder. I have performed baptisms, weddings, and funerals. I didn't do this as a practice, only when it was necessary. This training has affected the way I live my life.

I have been married to the same woman for sixty-one years. I have been home every night, except only when I was in the hospital or working. There was one night, some old friends of mine had been asking me to go coon hunting with them. I finally went. As we were sitting on a hill at about 2:00 a.m., and it was drizzling rain, we were listening to the dogs barking.

I thought, *Ain't nothing but a crazy person would do something like this.*

That was my first and last time to go coon hunting.

In addition to the work of the church that I was involved in, I also did other things. Since I was in the food business, everything that came up involving food also involved me. The biggest events required a lot of time and help. One was supper after vacation in Bible school. We would have a fish fry outside but eat it inside. I had a friend who had a gas-fired deep fryer. It was about the size of a bathtub. He was also a broker for a fish company. So he did the cooking. Ladies from church put the breading on the fish and passed them through the window. I handled getting all the things that we needed.

The other big event was we were one of the churches in middle Tennessee to host a Friday night singing. People from all around would assemble at one church each Friday night and sing until they got tired. They would take a break between nine and ten o'clock. The host would serve them with refreshments. We just fed them good. One of the things we served that they never saw any place else was a six-foot-long sub sandwich. At Robert Orr, we sold a six-foot-long loaf of bread. I would get two loafs, and we would slice it open with an electric knife. Then me and some help would put all of the ingredients in it. We would cover the box in aluminum foil and put the sandwich on top of the table and slice it with the electric knife. The people were amazed and ate both of them.

Another thing the church liked what I did was paint. When something needed painting, I wound up there. I think I have painted all of the Sunday school rooms, about fifteen of them, plus the small auditorium and the fellowship room. Along with Joe Adams, he and I painted the kitchen in the apartments.

Not all of my activities were done at the church. I went on several mission trips. The first one I remember was up to Eastern Kentucky to a rural town named Neon. It was close to Pikeville. We stayed at a new motel. It only had one double bed in the room, and we had two little girls. They both slept on a canvas cot, feet to feet. It had no air-conditioning in the mornings.

We conducted a vacation Bible school under a big tent. I was to organize the classes, so they would not interfere with each other. This was out in a big open field, so I had two classes under the tent far enough apart. I had one under a shade tree. One over by a stump and another over by a wrecked old car. After Bible school, we had lunch. After lunch, we knocked doors through the area. That place was really hilly. You could knock one door, look out back, and there was another house, look out back of that one and there was another house way up the hill. At about three o'clock, we had a radio program. And at night, we had church services at the church building.

Wille Jenkings had a van, and he drove through the community picking up children being relieved with nothing to do. They were glad to see us. We stayed the whole week. Everyone went home tired and happy. The next trip I took was to an island in the Caribbean Islands called Antigua. We had a mission preacher down there. I and three others went to encourage him and see what we could do to help him. That is a British island, and they spoke English, which was good. They had to import about all of their needs. We shipped a car for our man there to use, and there is a 100 percent traffic on any car coming in. This is to help pay for the roads which needed it. They also drive on the left side of the road. Everything was well and still is.

My next trip, a group of four of us went to Brownsville, Texas, where we were helping a church with its work in Mexico. That's the only time I ever spoke in an unknown tongue, which I joke with the people back home. They chose me to speak on Wednesday night, so I did. I spoke English to an audience of people who spoke Spanish, but I had a translator right beside me, telling them everything I said. We were there for a week and spent a lot of time in Mexico. It sure is different for such a short distance, but it was like that when I was in El Paso.

My family now consists of my wife and my three daughters. All are grown and have their own homes. But we are a little weird. I tell people we talk to each other. We usually have lunch together each Saturday. We have family gatherings, and we help each other when necessary.

I have made plans for them after I am gone. I realized that's a part of life. I have about used up all my birthdays.

CENTRAL PIKE CHURCH of CHRIST
Presented to
ROBERT DENNIS

FOR OUTSTANDING SERVICE WHILE
TEACHING GOD'S WORD.

40 PLUS YEARS

And the word of the Lord was being
spread throughout all the region.
Acts 13:49

CENTRAL PIKE CHURCH of CHRIST
Presented to
BARBARA DENNIS

FOR OUTSTANDING SERVICE WHILE
TEACHING GOD'S WORD TO OUR CHILDREN.

30 PLUS YEARS

And the word of the Lord was being
spread throughout all the region.
Acts 13:49

In the time of some of our travels, we have made some memories of incidents. When we were in Florida one summer at Mr. Nelson's house, I was fishing in the intercoastal waterways off his back yard. I was sitting under a shade tree with only my swimsuit on, but my feet were sticking out from under the shade, and they got sunburn. Now Barbara and the girls laughed at the picture of me diving into the swimming pool with my socks on.

Another time after Mr. Nelson turned all of the Kentucky State business over to me, I went up there every three months to see the people and check the bid results. Instead of flying and renting a car, I drove after much of the interstate was finished. Plus, Kentucky had a lot of toll roads just like the interstate. During the summer months when school was out, Barbara and the girls would go with me. We stayed at the Holiday Inn. I would go up in the afternoon before I visited the purchasing department the next day. Barbara and the girls would play in the park across the street while I was gone. On this trip, I had made contact with the person I dealt with at the purchasing department for him and his wife to have supper with us. He was a very conservative person. So while we were in the restaurant waiting for our table, he was sitting next to my six-year-old daughter, who was sitting next to me.

I heard him say, "Little girl, are you going to have a hamburger or a chicken leg?"

She said, "I am going to have prime rib."

I thought he would fall out of the chair. He was so surprised. We had traveled so much and so many places that the girls had learned to eat other things than hamburgers and chicken. I will always remember that evening, and that was fifty years ago.

Another event happened in California in the summer. We had a meeting in Los Angeles in July at the Century Plaza Hotel in Hollywood. I went out on Sunday; Barbara and the girls were coming out on Thursday. We were going to take a week's vacation after the meeting was over. Mr. Nelson and his wife would be there also. So before the meeting, we made some plans. The hotel had some three-room suites. It had two bedrooms with a parlor in between. He suggested we get that. He and his wife would have one bedroom, and me and my family in the other one, and the girls could play in the parlor. He and I worked the whole week, so on Thursday, after Barbara had gotten there, I went up to see if they were making it all right. It turned out not good. Susan had been running through the rooms, and she fell in the doorway and hit her head on the doorstop. She had cut a big gash in her forehead. Mrs. Nelson and Barbara had cleaned and patched her up but decided she should see a doctor. So we called the front desk and got a phone number and location and made an appointment. We took a taxi over there, which was close. The office was on the fourth floor. When we got up there, all the windows were open. The air conditioner was not working. It was hot outside and hot inside. They carried Susan back to the treatment room, wrapped her up in a sheet so she couldn't move, and began to sew up her head. Barbara went back there with her. After a few minutes, a nurse came out. She said, "You should come back and take care of your wife. She has fainted." Which I did. Susan was patched up again, and we went back to the hotel. You never know what is going to take place on one of these trips that you didn't plan for. We spent the next week with my aunt, and I don't remember where all we went on this trip.

I have not written this book to tell you how and what you should do but only to get you to think. If I did this, *you* can do better.

So God bless you for trying.

Very soon, I expect to have a cowriter working with me putting music to my songs, and then in the near future, we plan to make a lot of hits.

ABOUT THE AUTHOR

I was born in the mid-1930s in Nashville, Tennessee. My first five years, I grew up on my grandfather's farm in Kingston Springs, Tennessee, before my father was called back to work at the Workshop for the Blind in 1940, moving us back to Nashville. I went to school at Park Avenue School for a year and a half before our parents divorced. My younger brother, sister, and I were sent to the Fresh Air Camp for children located in Cheatham County…it was in the wilderness. We were there for two years. On December 3, 1943, we were foster kids living with the Bright family in rural Mount Juliet, on their farm. By the time I was a teenager, I was a regular farmhand—plowing the ground, hauling hay, taking care of the animals. I milked five cows before breakfast and again before supper. I lived there for the next ten years, finishing out my schooling.

My first job was at AVCO building airplanes and only lasted about two months before I got a job at Robert Orr company. They were a wholesale grocery distributing company, and I started out by typing invoices. A few years later, we moved into data processing equipment, and I worked there until the army got me. I spent three years in the army—two in Texas and one in Germany before heading back to Robert Orr. By that time, they had converted to a whole-sale food distributor. I worked several positions. One was the first national account executive, helping later in sales, then as the assistant to the vice president. My responsibilities increased, and I worked more in purchasing. In 1972 they became part of a public company called SYSCO. It has grown to be the largest in this country and several more. As time went on, I advanced to vice president of purchasing and merchandising of the Nashville location. During those years, I took several college courses just for my own learning, and I did a lot of traveling, learning a lot about financing. I retired at the end of 1999.

I've now been married for sixty-one years. We've raised three daughters, all of which went to college earning degrees, have initials after their name, and own their own homes. We are all a little weird. We talk to each other, have lunch together each Saturday, have family gatherings, and help each other when necessary. I have made plans for them after I am gone. I realize that is a part of life, and I've about used up all my birthdays.

CPSIA information can be obtained
at www.ICGtesting.com
Printed in the USA
BVHW040233170423
662367BV00003B/776